The Truth About TONGUES

Secrets Revealed Concerning the Baptism With the Holy Spirit

TONY SMITH

LITE Publishing
P.O. Box 581628
Elk Grove, CA 95758
www.litepublishing.com

Copyright © 2005, 2017 by Tony Smith

All rights reserved. Written permission must be secured from the publisher to use or reproduce any part of this book, except for brief quotations in critical reviews or articles.

Published in Elk Grove, California, by LITE Publishing

ISBN 978-0-9968298-0-9

Printed in the United States of America

Second Edition

TABLE OF CONTENTS

INTRODUCTION

God is not the author of confusion (1 Cor. 14:33). Yet mass confusion exists in the body of Christ today about speaking in tongues and the baptism with the Holy Spirit. Some believe that speaking in tongues is of the devil. Others believe that speaking in tongues is of God, but that not every believer can speak in tongues. Some people believe that every believer can speak in tongues, and that if you don't speak in tongues, you are not saved. Some people believe you have to tarry (wait) to receive the Holy Ghost. Some people believe the opposite. Other people don't know what to believe.

The confusion is understandable, to some degree. For one thing, different churches and different denominations teach about this subject differently. Adding to the confusion are the widely varied testimonies given by those who have been filled or say they have been filled with the Holy Spirit ("I saw a beam of light come down from the sky. . ." "It felt like a flood of water just ran right over me. . ." "I was driving down the highway praising God when all of a sudden. . ."). If that weren't enough, some people begin speaking in tongues before anyone ever ministers the baptism with the Holy Spirit to them, while others who do have the baptism with the Holy Spirit ministered to them never do speak in tongues. Some of those who do have the baptism with the Holy

Spirit ministered to them begin to speak in a fluent tongue immediately, while other people seem to have no immediate manifestation whatsoever. And some of the people who receive no manifestation insist that they have indeed been filled with the Holy Spirit, tongues or no tongues. And some who do speak in tongues live like the devil!

It's no wonder people are confused. Yet I am a firm believer that any person who continues in the Word of God will find out the truth, and that the truth will set that person free if he or she chooses to act on it (John 8:31-32). I have discovered in my Christian walk that the truth about ANYTHING will set you free, and the baptism with the Holy Spirit is no exception to the rule. This book should clear up any serious misconceptions you may have about the Holy Spirit and tongues, and it should eliminate any hindrances which have kept you in the dark about these subjects.

But before I go any further, a word of caution:

If we are ever going to grow and mature in our Christian walk, we have to get past the "itching ear" stage. The Bible talks about people who have "itching ears"—in other words, you have to tell these people what they want to hear or else they won't listen to you (2 Timothy 4:3). Some people have itching ears when it comes to tongues; they want the minister to tell them that speaking in tongues is of the devil, or that speaking in tongues is unimportant, or that speaking in tongues is not the initial evidence of the baptism with the

Holy Spirit, or that it's possible to be filled with the Holy Spirit without ever speaking in tongues. This gives them a legitimate excuse in their own minds not to speak in tongues.

Friend, that's the wrong attitude.

It isn't my job as a minister to tell you what you want to hear. My job is to speak the truth to you in love. There are times when I can speak the truth and tell you what you want to hear at the same time. Praise God for those times! But there are other times when the truth may not be what you wanted to hear. Even so, I encourage you to face the truth head on. Yield to it, and obey the direction given to you by the Word of God and by the Holy Spirit.

There is no point in you reading any further unless you are going to be serious in seeking the truth about the Holy Spirit and tongues. Make up your mind right now that you want the TRUTH about tongues and the baptism with the Holy Spirit—*regardless of whether it lines up with your preexisting beliefs.* If it has to line up with your preexisting beliefs before you will accept it, you are not serious about seeking the truth. Get serious about it! Do it now! Trust God! You'll discover that the truth will indeed set you free!

Now then, are you ready to be set free? If so, let's begin.

CHAPTER 1

Background on the Holy Spirit

Before we discuss the Holy Spirit baptism and tongues, it would be wise to offer some background information about the Holy Spirit Himself.

A very large book could be written about the Holy Spirit, but I am only planning to hit the high points in this chapter. You don't need to know everything about the Holy Spirit in order to receive Him, so I feel it would be unnecessary to discuss everything about the Holy Spirit from Genesis to Revelation. Nevertheless, because there is so much confusion in the body of Christ about the Holy Spirit, I believe it is necessary to give you at least a brief synopsis of the Holy Spirit and His role in the Christian life.

The Holy Spirit is the Third Person of the Godhead (Father, Son, and Holy Spirit). He is not an impersonal entity. He is a Person (John 14:26). He is also referred to as the Holy Ghost.

Jesus, speaking to his disciples prior to his death, burial, and resurrection, said he would pray to the Father, and that the Father would give the disciples another Comforter in place of Him, and that this Comforter would abide with them forever (John 14:16). This Comforter is referred to in the next verse as "the Spirit of Truth, whom the world cannot receive, because it seeth him not, neither knoweth him: but ye know him, for he dwelleth with you, and shall be in you."

In John 14:26, Jesus clarifies even further the identity of the Comforter, and sheds some more light on His purpose for the believer.

"But the Comforter, which is the Holy Ghost, whom the Father will send in my name, he shall teach you all things, and bring all things to your remembrance, whatsoever I have said unto you."

The Comforter, then, is the Holy Ghost, also known as the Holy Spirit.

In the fifteenth chapter of John, Jesus continues his discussion of the Holy Spirit by saying that when the Holy Spirit comes, He will testify of Jesus (John 15:26). In the sixteenth chapter of John, Jesus tells the disciples that in order for the Holy Spirit to come, Jesus must leave—an obvious reference to his death, burial, resurrection, and ascension to heaven (John 16:7). The next verse says that the Holy Spirit will come to convince (or convict) the world of sin, righteousness, and judgment. In verses 13 through 15, Jesus makes these statements:

"Howbeit when he, the Spirit of truth, is come, he will *guide you into all truth*: for he shall not speak of himself; but whatsoever he shall hear, that shall he speak: and he will *shew you things to come.*

"He shall *glorify me*: for he shall receive of mine, and shall shew it unto you.

"All things that the Father hath are mine: therefore said I, that he shall take of mine, and shall shew it unto you."

Before analyzing these scriptures any further, let's take another look at John 14:16, this time using the Amplified Bible, Classic Edition:

"And I will ask the Father, and He will give you another Comforter (Counselor, Helper, Intercessor, Advocate, Strengthener and Standby) that He may remain with you forever."

What Jesus was trying to communicate to his disciples, in a nutshell, is this:

"I am not going to be with you much longer. I am going away. You don't realize it yet, but I am going to die. I will be raised from the dead, and I will see you again. But even after I see you, I will ascend unto my Father in heaven. You are going to need another Comforter besides myself. My Father and I will send you another Comforter. He is the Holy Ghost.

"He will be your Comforter. He will be your Counselor, or guide. He will be your Helper. He will be your Intercessor when you pray. He will be your Advocate when the devil tries to accuse you. He will be your Strengthener in times when you lack strength. He will be your Standby. He will never leave you, nor forsake you. He will be your Teacher. He will cause you to remember My words even when I am not with you. He will convince the world of sin, righteousness, and judgment. He will show you things to come. He will glorify Me. *And He will dwell in you.*"

At the time Jesus spoke in this manner to the disciples, the Holy Spirit had not yet come. But the Holy Spirit is here on the earth today. And as you can see from Jesus' extensive description, the Holy Spirit is a very busy Person. He takes a very, very active role in the life of a believer.

It isn't required that you memorize all the things that the Holy Spirit does for the Christian. The main thing that you need to understand right now—the main thing that you should be able to sense from the words of Jesus—is that it is impossible to live a victorious Christian life without the aid of the Holy Spirit. For any Christian to think that they can live the Christian life on this planet without the assistance of the Holy Spirit is foolishness. It is the ultimate act of pride for a Christian to snub the Holy Spirit. It is like telling Jesus "Thank you for sending the Holy Spirit, but no thanks. I don't need Him. I can make it on my own."

If you actually can make it on your own, without the aid of the Holy Spirit, someone forgot to tell Jesus. Jesus seems to think otherwise, if His words are any indication. According to Jesus, you *do* need the Holy Spirit. Why would he have sent the Holy Spirit if we *didn't* need Him?

Jesus addressed the need for the Holy Spirit in Acts 1:8, when he said:

"But ye shall receive power, *after the Holy Ghost is come upon you*: and ye shall be witnesses unto me both in Jerusalem, and in all Judaea, and in Samaria, and unto the uttermost part of the earth."

When did Jesus say the disciples would receive power?

After the Holy Ghost came upon them. Not before.

The word "power" in the original Greek means "divine ability." Jesus said the disciples would receive "divine ability" *after* the Holy Ghost came upon them. In other words, they would not receive this "divine ability" before the Holy Ghost came upon them. Then in Acts 2, we see the Holy Ghost come upon the disciples. And the rest is history.

The main point I am trying to make right now is that the Holy Spirit is a source of supernatural power for the believer. And Jesus implied that you NEED this power. The Holy Spirit is a Strengthener, because He adds "divine ability" to your natural ability. We will discuss this later in more detail.

There is much more to say about the Holy Spirit than I can say here. But this brief overview should be enough to show you how important the Holy Spirit is in the life of a believer. Now that we have laid some groundwork, let us begin to address the issue of the baptism with the Holy Spirit, which Jesus referred to in Acts 1:4-5. He said:

". . .Wait for *the promise of the Father*, which, saith he, ye have heard of me.

"For John truly baptized with water, but ye shall be *baptized with the Holy Ghost* not many days hence."

CHAPTER 2

The Doctrine of Baptisms

"Therefore leaving the principles of the doctrine of Christ, let us go on unto perfection; not laying again the foundation of repentance from dead works, and of faith toward God,

"Of the DOCTRINE OF BAPTISMS, and of laying on of hands, and of resurrection of the dead, and of eternal judgment." –

Hebrews 6:1-2

In order to discuss the baptism with the Holy Ghost in an intelligent manner, I feel as though I must first define what baptism is and then establish the biblical fact that there is more than one type of baptism.

The word "baptism" comes from a Greek word that means "to immerse" or "to make fully wet." It does not mean "to sprinkle." It means "to immerse." To immerse literally means "to submerge" or "to plunge (something or someone) into (a liquid)."

Notice that the word "baptism" appears in the plural in the above passage in Hebrews. This indicates that there is more than one type of baptism. Even if the word appeared in the singular in this verse, other scriptures in the Bible also provide solid evidence for the concept of more than one baptism. For example:

"For John truly baptized with water; but ye shall be baptized with the Holy Ghost not many days hence." – Acts 1:5

This passage clearly makes reference to two different types of baptism, not just one.

Friend, if you ever want to discover the truth about the Holy Spirit, you must understand that there is more than one baptism available to you. As Hebrews 6:1-2 indicates, the doctrine of baptisms (plural) is a foundational doctrine of Christ. In other words, we are dealing with basic truths here.

Why then is there so much confusion about this in the body of Christ? One reason for this is because one scripture in the Bible (Ephesians 4:5) has been widely misinterpreted. Let's take a look at it in its immediate context:

"There is one body, and one Spirit, even as ye are called in one hope of your calling;

"One Lord, one faith, ONE BAPTISM,

"One God and Father of all, who is above all, and through all, and in you all."- Ephesians 4:4-6

Some people have assumed from this passage that there is only one type of baptism (usually they will say it is water baptism). These same people will say that unless you are water baptized, you cannot be saved. This is unscriptural.

The Bible is clear: you are saved by grace only, not by works (Ephesians 2:8-9; Galatians 2:16). You are saved by Jesus only, not by some minister who dunks you in water. If water baptism were needed for salvation, the thief on the cross would have been destined for hell and the lake of fire. Jesus, however, said otherwise: *"Verily I say unto thee, Today shalt thou be with me in PARADISE" (Luke 23:43).*

Water baptism is scriptural, but salvation by water baptism is not. Moreover, to believe in salvation by water baptism, you must believe one scripture at the expense of other scriptures. This violates a commonsense rule of Bible interpretation: *when faced with two scriptures that are seemingly contradictory, don't assume that one scripture is true and the other false. Assume that they are both true.* The Bible, after all, is the Word of Truth.

If you look at one verse (Hebrews 6:2), it appears as though there is more than one kind of baptism. Look at another verse (Ephesians 4:5), and it appears as though there is only one. Which one is correct? Both.

How can that be? Well, first of all, *assume* they are both true. Once you make the decision that you are going to believe the whole Bible even when you don't understand portions of it, that opens the door for God to speak to you and reveal divine secrets to you.

Hebrews 6:2 speaks of more than one baptism. Acts 1:5

also speaks of more than one baptism. And the Bible says that in the mouth of two or three witnesses every word should be established (Matthew 18:16). At least two scriptures (actually there are more than two) say there is more than one kind of baptism. Therefore, we have a legitimate basis for saying there is more than one kind of baptism.

One scripture (Ephesians 4:5) says there is ONE baptism. I know of no other scripture which clearly gives the same indication. Even so, we know by faith that this scripture is true. But if we conclude from this that there is ONLY ONE baptism, we have to ignore any scriptures that say otherwise. *When you start ignoring scriptures to preserve your own beliefs, you are bound to get off into error.*

Hebrews 6:2 is true. Ephesians 4:5 is true. Both scriptures are true. Ephesians 4:5 says there is ONE baptism. It does not say there is ONLY ONE baptism. It says there is ONE baptism. Taken in context with the rest of the Bible, this means that ONE baptism must be more important than all OTHER baptisms.

This is true. One baptism is more important than the others. But it isn't water baptism. Nor is it the baptism with the Holy Spirit.

For the sake of this study, we are going to look at *three* different kinds of baptism mentioned in the Bible, starting with the most important (and most overlooked) one.

1. Baptism into the body of Christ (the new birth) —

What? Are you trying to say the new birth is a baptism? I'm not *trying* to say anything; I'm just coming right out and *saying* it, praise God! *The new birth is a baptism.* More accurately, it can be called "baptism into the body of Christ."

"For by one Spirit are we ALL baptized into one body, whether we be Jews or Gentiles, whether we be bond or free; and have been ALL made to drink into one Spirit." – 1 Corinthians 12:13

Many people, when they read this verse, think it is referring to water baptism. But we really have no clear basis to reach that conclusion. As we discussed earlier, the word "baptize" means "to immerse." It does not necessarily mean "to immerse *with water.*" Not every Biblical reference to baptism is referring to water baptism. Since the scripture makes no mention of water here, we have no basis to assume that this has anything to do with water.

If you look at this passage closely, you will discover that it is talking about the new birth, which is also referred to in the Bible as being "born of the Spirit" (John 3:6, 8). Notice that it says "For by one Spirit are we ALL baptized into one body." Not some of us. ALL of us. ALL of us Christians, that is. All Christians are not water-baptized, although they should be. All Christians are not baptized with the Holy Spirit. But all Christians are, by definition, baptized (immersed) into the body of Christ (that is, born again).

Keep this in mind—in order to have a baptism, you must

have three things present: first, a baptizer; secondly, a person who is being baptized; and thirdly, an element for them to be baptized in or baptized into. Using this formula, we can make sense out of this scripture passage and see that it is really referring to salvation.

The baptizer, in this case, is the Holy Spirit ("For BY ONE SPIRIT are we all baptized"). The person being baptized, in this case, is the person receiving salvation—remember, it is the Holy Spirit's job to convince people in the world of their sin and their need for righteousness, that they may be saved (John 16:8). The element into which the person is baptized, in this case, is the body of Christ!

Doesn't that make sense, though? When you receive Jesus Christ as Savior, you become a new creature in Christ (2 Cor. 5:17). How? The Holy Spirit baptizes (or immerses) your sinful nature into the cleansing waters of Christ's body, purifying your heart and making you brand new on the inside! And you become a part of the universal body of Christ, which is the church! Hallelujah!

So the new birth is indeed a baptism. And it is the *most important* kind of baptism. It is the "One Baptism" being referred to Ephesians 4:5. For without it, you can't be saved. Unless you are baptized into the body of Christ, water baptism won't do you any good. Unless you are baptized into the body of Christ, the baptism with the Holy Spirit is not even an option. Unless you are baptized into the body of Christ, you cannot see the kingdom of heaven (John 3:3).

The terms "baptized into the body of Christ," "baptized into Jesus," "born of the Spirit," and "born again" are synonyms. They basically all mean the same thing. They are all referring to the new birth and what happens at the new birth.

Once you have been baptized into the body of Christ by receiving Jesus Christ as your Savior and Lord (Romans 10:8-9), you are now eligible for water baptism.

2. Water baptism—Water baptism was practiced by John the Baptist, who was a forerunner to Jesus (John 1:26). After Jesus' death, the disciples continued to baptize new believers in water (Acts 19:4-5; Acts 8:35-38; Acts 10:47), setting a New Testament pattern for us to follow today.

Remember that there are three elements to baptism: the baptizer, the "baptizee," and the element into which the person is baptized. With water baptism, the baptizer is the preacher. The "baptizee"—the person being baptized—is the new believer. The element into which the person is being baptized is water.

Water baptism has been called "an outward sign of an inward grace." It is an outward demonstration of what has already happened inwardly. It is actually a symbolic representation of the first baptism we discussed—the baptism into the body of Christ (Romans 6:3-4).

The entire process of the believer being immersed in water and then subsequently raised up out of the water is symbolic of several things, including the death, burial, and resurrection of Christ. But it is also symbolic of your death, burial, and resurrection, if you are a Christian. According to the scriptures, your old sinful nature has been crucified with Christ (Galatians 2:20, Romans 6:6); you were subsequently buried with Christ (Romans 6:4); and now you have been raised from the dead with Christ (Ephesians 2:6). Glory to God!

While water baptism is not a requirement for salvation, every believer who is able to do so should experience water baptism. All believers should want to publicly identify with Jesus' death, burial, and resurrection, as well as with their own death, burial, and resurrection in Christ.

3. Baptism with the Holy Spirit – Let us first recall the words of John the Baptist in Luke 3:16.

". . .I indeed baptize you with water; but one mightier than I cometh, the latchet of whose shoes I am not worthy to unloose: he shall BAPTIZE YOU WITH THE HOLY GHOST and WITH FIRE:"

We are discussing the baptism with the Holy Ghost. So without going any further, let's establish who the baptizer is, who the "baptizee" is, and what element is being used for baptism. We understand that John the Baptist's mission in life was to prepare the way for the coming Messiah, that is,

Jesus. In light of that, Luke 3:16 indicates that *Jesus* is the baptizer. The believer in Jesus is the "baptizee." The element into which the believer is baptized is the Holy Ghost.

What about the "fire," which is mentioned at the end of the verse? We'll discuss that a little later. First we must establish a few truths concerning the baptism with the Holy Spirit.

Let's go back for a minute to Acts 1:4-5, where Jesus says:

". . .Wait for *the promise of the Father*, which, saith he, ye have heard of me.

"For John truly baptized with water, but ye shall be *baptized with the Holy Ghost* not many days hence."

Notice here that "the promise of the Father" is another name for being "baptized with the Holy Ghost."

This was NOT a reference to the new birth. If believing in a risen Saviour is a requirement for being born again (Romans 10:9), then the disciples indeed experienced the new birth shortly after the resurrection of Jesus. Remember when Jesus breathed on the disciples and said "receive ye the Holy Ghost" (John 20:22). In all likelihood, it was at this point when the Holy Ghost baptized the disciples into the body of Christ, and they actually experienced the new birth. But I'm not going to be dogmatic about it. Even if they *didn't* experience the new birth at the precise moment that Jesus breathed on them, there is a general consensus in Christian circles that Peter, John, Matthew, and the rest of the disciples were indeed Christians by this time, if not beforehand.

In other words, Jesus is speaking to born-again believers here in Acts 1:4-5 when he tells them to "wait for the promise of the Father." So the "promise of the Father" in this case is NOT the new birth, since that has already occurred. The promise is referred to in Acts 1:5 as *the baptism with the Holy Ghost.*

Think about that a second. That is a very significant point which contradicts some traditional teaching about the Holy Spirit.

There are some people who will tell you that the baptism with the Holy Ghost occurred in John 20 when Jesus breathed on the disciples and said "receive ye the Holy Ghost." This is a popular passage used by denominations and church groups who do not fully embrace the concept of speaking in tongues. Since speaking in tongues is not mentioned in John 20, some groups use John 20 as a proof text to illustrate their assertion that the baptism with the Holy Spirit isn't necessarily related to speaking in tongues.

If that is true, why did Jesus—in his last minutes on earth just before his ascension to heaven—tell the disciples in Acts 1:4-5 to "wait for the promise of the Father...ye shall be baptized with the Holy Spirit not many days hence"? Apparently the baptism with the Holy Spirit had not yet occurred, even though he is making this statement AFTER

John 20.

Moreover, Jesus' last words before ascending to heaven (Acts 1:8) were still referring to this Holy Ghost experience in the FUTURE tense: "But ye *shall* receive power, after that the Holy Ghost is come upon you: and ye shall be witnesses…" One verse later, Jesus is taken up to heaven in a cloud, and *the disciples still don't have the power. Yet.*

Is this unusual? No. Not when you consider what Jesus said in John 16:7: ". . .for IF I GO NOT AWAY, the Comforter will NOT COME unto you; but IF I DEPART, I WILL SEND HIM UNTO YOU." In Acts 1:9, Jesus departs. In Acts 2, the Holy Spirit is sent. With supernatural signs following.

"And when the day of Pentecost was fully come, they were all with one accord in one place.

"And suddenly there came a sound from heaven as of a rushing mighty wind, and it filled all the house where they were sitting.

"And there appeared unto them cloven tongues like as of FIRE, and it sat upon each of them (Remember that John the Baptist said they would be baptized with the Holy Ghost and with FIRE.).

"And they were ALL FILLED WITH THE HOLY GHOST, and BEGAN TO SPEAK WITH OTHER TONGUES, as the Spirit gave them utterance." – Acts 2:1-4

There is more than one reference to the baptism with

the Holy Ghost in the book of Acts, but only one of them mentions fire, and that is here. Even in this case, it is not a literal fire ("cloven tongues LIKE AS OF fire"). The "fire" was a supernatural sign to these early believers that the first instance of the baptism with the Holy Spirit was indeed happening before their very eyes. There is no mention of this "fire" after Acts 2:3. The "baptism with fire" is a symbolic reference to the baptism with the Holy Spirit.

So let's do a quick review. Jesus tells the disciples in Acts 1 to wait for the promise of the Father, which is the baptism with the Holy Spirit. In Acts 2, the baptism with the Holy Spirit occurs. And, according to Acts 2:4, ALL of the believers in the upper room are filled with the Holy Ghost, with the evidence of speaking with other tongues.

Isn't it interesting that ALL of the believers were filled with the Holy Ghost? Isn't it interesting that ALL of the believers present began to speak with tongues? Isn't it interesting that NONE of the believers went home empty? ALL of them were filled, and ALL of them had supernatural evidence to confirm it!

Is this just a fluke, or is this supposed to be a biblical pattern for experiencing the baptism with the Holy Spirit? Let us look at the baptism with the Holy Spirit in greater detail. Let us see what the rest of the book of Acts has to say about it. Let us make an honest search for the truth.

CHAPTER 3

Are Tongues Part of the Baptism?

We learned in the last chapter about different types of baptism, and we began to discuss an experience that occurs after salvation called the baptism with the Holy Spirit. Our focus had turned to Acts 2:4, which tells of what happened when the Holy Ghost fell on the disciples in the upper room.

"And they were ALL FILLED WITH THE HOLY GHOST, and BEGAN TO SPEAK WITH OTHER TONGUES, as the Spirit gave them utterance." – Acts 2:4

This raises a question: are tongues part of the package? Does the baptism with the Holy Spirit necessarily involve speaking in tongues? This question has been a continuous source of debate and disagreement. And yet the answers to such questions are in the Bible. Most of them are in the book of Acts.

Let us see if there are any other references to the baptism with the Holy Spirit in the book of Acts.

In Acts Chapter 10, Peter is preaching the word of salvation to Cornelius and other Gentiles in Caesarea. As they hear the word and believe it, an interesting thing happens.

"While Peter yet spake these words, the Holy Ghost fell on all them which heard the word.

"And they of the circumcision which believed were astonished, as many as came with Peter, because that on the Gentiles also was poured out the gift of the Holy Ghost.

"For they heard them SPEAK WITH TONGUES, and magnify God. Then answered Peter,

"Can any man forbid water, that these should not be baptized, WHICH HAVE RECEIVED THE HOLY GHOST as well as we?

"And he commanded them to be baptized in the name of the Lord. Then prayed they him to tarry certain days." – Acts 10:44-48

Here is another reference to the baptism with the Holy Ghost. *And the initial outward sign that the baptism had occurred was that they spoke in tongues.* Acts 10:47 clearly implies that speaking in tongues is a sign that a believer has indeed "received the Holy Ghost." In fact, speaking in tongues is the only sign mentioned here.

Before I go any further, let us quickly deal with the issue of "receiving the Holy Ghost." We have seen this term already used in John 20, but here it is used differently. In this case, it is clearly referring to the baptism with the Holy Spirit. So when you see the phrase "receiving the Holy Ghost" in the Bible, what it means depends on the context.

If there is any doubt as to whether Acts 10 is referring to the baptism with the Holy Spirit, Peter removes all doubt in Acts 11 when he retells the story of what happened in Caesarea. Let's pick up on what Peter was saying at verse 15:

"And as I began to speak, THE HOLY GHOST FELL ON THEM, <u>AS ON US AT THE BEGINNING</u>.

"Then remembered I the word of the Lord, how that he said, John indeed baptized with water, but YE SHALL BE BAPTIZED WITH THE HOLY GHOST." – Acts 11:15-16

Peter very plainly states that what happened to the Gentiles at Caesarea was the same thing that happened to him and the other disciples on the day of Pentecost, which was the baptism with the Holy Spirit.

In Acts 19, Paul finds some disciples in Ephesus and poses a question to them: "Have you received the Holy Ghost since you believed?" (Acts 19:2). Here we see another variation of the phrase "receiving the Holy Ghost," and for the second time it is clearly referring to the baptism with the Holy Spirit. It couldn't be referring to salvation; otherwise Paul was actually asking the disciples a redundant question: "Have you believed since you believed?" No, "receiving the Holy Ghost" in this case is the same as "the baptism with the Holy Ghost." The baptism takes place in Acts 19:6.

"And when Paul had laid his hands upon them, THE HOLY GHOST CAME ON THEM; and they SPAKE WITH TONGUES, and PROPHESIED."

I don't know about you, but I see a very clear pattern here. Any time you have the baptism with the Holy Spirit taking place, the recipients are speaking with tongues. In this case, they were not only speaking with tongues, but prophesying!

By this time, we can safely conclude that speaking in tongues is a sign that a person has been baptized with the Holy Spirit. By all indications, it is the initial outward sign. Even though Acts 19:6 mentions "prophesying" as an additional sign, *tongues are mentioned first*. In fact, there are no recorded instances in the Book of Acts of anyone being baptized with the Holy Spirit who didn't speak with tongues.

Don't get me wrong. There are some recorded incidents of the baptism with the Holy Spirit which *do not mention* tongues (Acts 9:17, Acts 8:15-19). But even in these cases, speaking in tongues is implied.

For example, Paul was filled with the Holy Spirit in Acts Chapter 9, and it doesn't say he spoke with tongues. Yet in 1 Corinthians 14:18, Paul says "I thank my God, I SPEAK WITH TONGUES MORE THAN YE ALL." When did he start doing that? Surely not when he was known as Saul. Surely not when he was persecuting the church. In all likelihood, it started when Ananias laid hands on him to be filled with the Holy Spirit in Acts 9:17.

In Acts Chapter 8, Peter and John laid hands on believers in Samaria that they might receive the Holy Ghost. It doesn't say they spoke with tongues. But whatever happened was not just a wonderful spiritual blessing; it was something which was *visible* and could be perceived by the senses. In fact, it so captivated the attention of a former sorcerer named Simon that he offered Peter and John money that he might have the same power to lay hands on people to receive the Holy Ghost. Peter rebuked Simon, of course, but my point is this: why would a former sorcerer—someone who has had experience in supernatural things—offer Peter and John money to get the same power that they had? This only makes sense if you conclude that the power that Peter and John had was *clearly supernatural,* and that there was some sort of *outward manifestation* displayed by the recipients. Speaking in tongues is indeed an outward manifestation, and it is supernatural.

The overall evidence, my friend, strongly suggests that speaking in tongues is the initial outward evidence of the baptism with the Holy Spirit. You don't have to take my word for it. If you are so led, feel free to search the scriptures for yourself. Make a honest search for the truth. However, I am persuaded that an honest search for the truth will only lead to one conclusion: *speaking with tongues is the initial outward evidence of the baptism with the Holy Spirit.*

Some of you may have already noticed something, however. I keep saying "initial outward evidence." Most pastors and teachers in charismatic Christian circles will tell you that speaking in tongues is the initial evidence of the baptism with the Holy Spirit. *This is true, but it can be misleading.* It is especially misleading to Christians who have the baptism with the Holy Spirit ministered to them, but don't receive a fluent tongue. They have a tendency to think that because they aren't speaking in tongues the way they thought they would, that they have not received the Holy Spirit. *This isn't necessarily true.*

What we need to understand is that there are two types of evidence which can be discussed here—*outward* and *inward*. We are talking in this chapter about speaking in tongues, which is the *initial outward evidence* of being filled with the Holy Ghost. But there is also the *initial inward evidence* that you have received the Holy Ghost, and the inward evidence generally comes <u>before</u> the outward evidence! We will discuss this in more detail in the next chapter. Stay tuned!

CHAPTER 4

Can I Receive the Holy Ghost Without the Tongues?

We concluded the last chapter by asserting that speaking in tongues is the initial outward evidence of the baptism with the Holy Spirit. This, of course, raises the question: Is it possible to receive the Holy Spirit without the initial outward evidence of speaking in tongues?

If you were raised in Pentecostal or charismatic Christian circles, you may be expecting a "No" answer to this question. But I'm a firm believer that you should not believe anything just because someone else believes it; you should believe it *because it lines up with the Word of God.* Does the Bible give any hint or indication that it is possible to receive the Holy Spirit without initially speaking in a fluent tongue?

Yes, it does.

"What?"

You heard me. I said "Yes, it does."

First, allow me to clarify what I mean. It is true that the Bible gives no specific instances of a Christian who was baptized with the Holy Ghost who didn't speak with tongues (we'll discuss this more later). Even though this is true, the Bible does offer a general principle which offers great hope to those people who have been earnestly seeking the baptism with the Holy Spirit, but have no discernible "tongue" to show for it. One place where this hope can be found is in Hebrews 11:1.

"Now FAITH is the substance of things hoped for; THE EVIDENCE OF THINGS NOT SEEN."

This passage says that *faith* is the evidence of things not seen. In other words, faith is the proof—the *inward* evidence—that the things you are believing God for (things not yet seen) will manifest in your life. To shed further light on this passage, let's look at Hebrews 11:1 in the Amplified Bible, Classic Version:

"Now FAITH is the assurance (the confirmation, the title deed) of the things [we] hope for, being the PROOF of things [we] do not see and the CONVICTION OF THEIR REALITY [faith PERCEIVING AS REAL FACT WHAT IS NOT REVEALED TO THE SENSES]."

For those of who may have a hard time understanding or grasping the concept of faith, the last portion of Hebrews 11:1 sheds a great deal of light on it: *faith perceives as real fact what is not yet revealed to the senses.*

Before showing how this applies to the baptism with the Holy Spirit, let's see how this principle is applied in our everyday life:

A man (Joe Jones) with an impressive resume is laid off from his job, and for reasons beyond his control, has been out of work for eight months. Finally, a major corporation hires Joe as a district manager. The human resources manager tells Joe that he will get his first paycheck in two weeks.

As you might expect, Joe is thrilled. He goes home, kisses his wife and kids, gives them the good news, and offers to take them all out to Red Lobster for dinner! He begins making plans on what he is going to do with his first check. His wife also begins making plans on what to do with the money!

The bottom line is that Joe and his wife are happy. Joe and his wife are expectant. Joe and his wife are more confident about their future. Why? *Because Joe and his wife are perceiving as real fact what is not yet revealed to their senses!*

Say what?

Well, think about it. What if the human resources manager was lying? What if he was telling the truth at the time, but the company went out of business just prior to his first day of employment? What if a nuclear bomb destroyed the world in three days? I realize the nuclear bomb example is highly unlikely, but I hope you are seeing my point. The point is that it is humanly possible that Joe will not get his paycheck. If the corporation that hired him is a stable one which has been around for a while, it is highly unlikely that Joe will not get a paycheck. *But it is possible.*

Yet Joe and his wife aren't thinking about that possibility.

Instead, they are happy, expectant, and confident about their future, *all because of what one man said. Joe has no paycheck in his hands; the money has not yet been revealed to his senses.* And yet Joe and his wife are already making plans on what to do with that money, even though the only proof that they will receive any money is one man's word. Joe and his wife are perceiving his regular paycheck as a REAL FACT even though it hasn't manifested yet. Not surprisingly, two weeks later (and every two weeks after that), their faith is rewarded.

Keep in mind, we're not even talking about Bible faith in this example. We're discussing how natural human faith operates. Yet Bible faith operates in a similar manner. *Bible faith perceives as real fact what is not yet revealed to the senses.* But there is one major difference between natural human faith and Bible faith: natural human faith is based on the word of a man, which may or may not be trustworthy; while Bible faith is based on the word of Jesus Christ, the Son of God, making it completely trustworthy! Glory to God!

Now, let's apply that principle to the baptism with the Holy Spirit.

Let's say you are a Christian who has never been filled with the Holy Spirit. You attend a service where an invitation is extended for those who would like to receive the Holy Ghost. You are taken to a room and taught about the Holy Spirit; then the baptism with the Holy Spirit is ministered to you. You yield to the Holy Ghost as much as possible, based on the knowledge you have at the time. You believe you are receiving the Holy Spirit. Yet as you attempt to speak in an unknown tongue, what comes out of your mouth sounds like. . .nothing. At its best, it sounds like unintelligible noise. It certainly doesn't sound like a language. What do you do?

Well, you could do what many Christians have done—assume that because you aren't speaking in a fluent tongue, that you didn't receive the Holy Spirit. Instead of going that route, however, allow me to suggest another approach.

Start by asking yourself this question: did you receive?

"Well, I'm not speaking in tongues like I thought I would be."

That's not what I asked you. I asked you "Did you *receive*?"

"Huh?"

Forget about tongues for a minute. Let's put the "tongues" issue on the shelf for now. Tongues are not the issue right now. *Receiving* is the issue. Do not use the "speaking in tongues" issue to determine whether you have received the Holy Spirit. *Receiving the Holy Spirit and speaking in tongues are not the same thing. They are related, but they are not the same thing.* So forget about tongues right now. Let's deal with this issue—to receive or not to receive.

Did you receive? Were you in a receiving mode? Did you welcome the Holy Spirit into your heart? Were you open to receiving Him? Or did you reject Him? Were you willing to yield yourself to the Third Person of the Godhead coming to live on the inside of you? Or did pride or fear cause you to resist the Holy Ghost? Did you receive fully? Or did you start to receive, and then stop because of fear or pride? Did you receive on your terms, or on God's terms?

I'm not asking ten different questions here; I'm just asking one question ten different ways: Did you *receive*?

"Well, now that you put it that way, I did receive. But maybe I didn't receive fully."

Now you are on the right track! *Remember that Bible faith perceives as real fact what is not yet revealed to the senses.* If you received at all – if you believe you received the Holy Spirit in any measure – then consider it a REAL FACT that you have indeed been filled with the Holy Spirit, even if the "fluent tongue" has not yet been revealed to your senses! Consider yourself a Spirit-filled believer!

"You mean that it is possible for a person to be filled with the Holy Spirit and not speak with tongues?"

No, I didn't say that. *Truth be told, it is almost <u>impossible</u> for a person who is filled with the Spirit not to speak with tongues.*

"What? You're contradicting yourself! I'm confused! Before, you said it was possible; now you're saying it's almost impossible!"

It's not a contradiction. But follow me very closely here.

What I'm about to say is very important. Your understanding of it may be a crucial factor in determining whether you are ever filled with the Holy Spirit or not.

It is POSSIBLE for a person who has *received* the Holy Spirit to <u>not</u> speak in a fluent tongue. But it is almost IMPOSSIBLE for a person who is *filled* or *baptized* with the Spirit to <u>not</u> speak in a fluent tongue. If you are truly filled to overflowing with the Holy Spirit, it is all you can do to keep from speaking in tongues! You practically have to shut your mouth and glue your lips together to keep from doing it. And believe it or not, that's what some people do. They shouldn't, but because they don't know better, they do.

Some of you who have been taught differently may believe that I have totally missed it here. But I'm not teaching some new doctrine. It is merely a biblical principle (faith perceiving as fact what has not yet been revealed to the senses), combined with spiritual common sense and an understanding of what three words mean. Those three words are *received, filled,* and *baptized.*

All three of these words are used in the Bible in connection with the Holy Spirit, and they are often used interchangeably. However, if you look up these words in the dictionary, they do not mean exactly the same thing. There are different shades of meaning to these words, and we need to examine them closely in order to understand them.

Perhaps the best way to do that is by using an illustration.

CHAPTER 5

Received, Filled, and Baptized

At least three terms are used to describe the experience subsequent to salvation involving the Holy Spirit. These terms are as follows: *received* the Holy Ghost, *filled* with the Holy Ghost, and *baptized* with the Holy Ghost.

Because these terms are used interchangeably in the Bible, it is commonly taught that they all mean the same thing. Webster's Dictionary, however, does not use the same definition for the words *receive, fill,* and *baptize*. These are three different words with three different meanings. The words are not opposites, but they are different.

Perhaps the best way to see the difference between these three words is to use an illustration involving a glass of water. Once we understand the illustration of the water, it will help us to better understand how these three words apply to the baptism with the Holy Ghost.

Take a large bucket and put a small 12-ounce glass in the middle of the bucket. Put an Alka-Seltzer tablet in the glass. Fill the glass up with water until it begins to overflow. If you continue to pour the water, it will not only immerse the glass in water, but it will fill the bucket with water as well! *In this case, the glass has received water; it has been filled with water; and it has been immersed (or baptized) in water.* All three things have occurred.

This is a perfect illustration of what happens (or what should happen) when a person is baptized with the Holy Spirit. A person *receives* the Holy Spirit and continues to receive until the point at which he is *filled* to overflowing with the Holy Spirit, and at this point the process of being immersed in (or *baptized* with) the Holy Spirit has begun. This entire process can occur instantaneously. In fact, this was the normal pattern experienced by New Testament believers in the early church, as recorded in the Book of Acts. And this is why the three terms are used interchangeably in the New Testament.

The process can still occur instantaneously today, but too often it doesn't. The devil is a major contributor to this disturbing trend. We know (or should know) that the devil is a defeated foe, and he ultimately can't stop the work of God from being accomplished in the earth. Even so, Satan has done a lot to hinder the work of God, particularly when it comes to the baptism with the Holy Spirit.

You see, the devil was not pleased at all at the Day of Pentecost. He was not pleased at all when multitudes of believers suddenly began receiving the Holy Spirit with the supernatural evidence of tongues, because it meant that these believers were receiving the divine ability to defeat all the power of the enemy in their lives. Satan knew that if his kingdom were to prosper on the earth, he would have to stop the momentum being generated by the rise of Spirit-filled, tongue-talking Christians. And over the years, he has had a great deal of success in causing confusion and strife over the "tongues" issue and the baptism with the Holy Ghost. He has influenced many preachers to unwittingly tell lies from the pulpit about tongues and the baptism with the Holy Ghost. He has fought "speaking in tongues" tooth-and-nail for close to 2,000 years.

One of the byproducts of this fight is that many Christians have been so "religiously brainwashed" by false or watered-down doctrine that it is difficult for them to receive the Holy Spirit at all. Or if they do receive, they only receive *in part*. So instead of having a full bucket, with a glass full of water, all we have is a glass which is half full, or one-third of the way full. The glass has indeed *received* water, but it hasn't been *filled* with water.

According to Acts 2:4, speaking in tongues is not the first thing that happens after you *receive* the Holy Spirit. Speaking in tongues is the first thing that happens after you are *filled* with the Spirit.

"And they were all FILLED with the Holy Ghost, and BEGAN TO SPEAK WITH OTHER TONGUES as the Spirit gave them utterance." – Acts 2:4.

So, just as it is possible for a glass to receive water, but

not be filled with water, so it is also possible for a person to receive the Holy Spirit, but not be filled with the Holy Spirit. And if you are not filled with the Holy Spirit, you will not be able to speak in a fluent tongue as the Holy Spirit gives you the utterance. Doesn't that make sense?

Why am I making this distinction? *Because hidden in this distinction are the secrets which will make a difference between whether a chronic seeker ever experiences the baptism with the Holy Spirit in its fullness or not.*

Some people repeatedly ask for prayer for the baptism with the Holy Spirit. They travel from church to church, from minister to minister, from meeting to meeting. Yet they always seem to come away empty. Why?

One of the main reasons why is this: they usually make the incorrect assumption that because they are not speaking in a fluent tongue, that they did not *receive*. In many cases, that isn't necessarily true. They *did* receive. They just weren't *filled*. Because when you are filled to overflowing with the Holy Spirit, speaking in a fluent tongue is pretty much automatic. All you have to do is open your mouth and let that supernatural language come out! You don't have to work at it; it just flows.

"But what do I do if I have received, but I'm not yet filled?"

Keep receiving until you ARE filled!

You don't have to worry about whether God will pour

out His Spirit upon you, or whether He will continue to pour out His Spirit until you are filled. God already poured out the Holy Ghost on the day of Pentecost, and He's been in the earth realm ever since! It's not up to God to give you the Holy Spirit; it's up to you to receive the Holy Spirit. And once you've started receiving, don't stop! Don't stop just because you don't have a fluent tongue yet. If someone is praying with you to be filled, and by the time they are done praying, you still aren't speaking in a fluent tongue, don't get discouraged. If you received at all (even if you are like a glass that is only one-tenth of the way full), *then you have indeed received.* Don't stop believing just because you have no fluent tongue.

Remember, faith perceives as real fact what is not yet revealed to the senses. **It is a fact that you have received. But if you aren't speaking in a fluent tongue, it is not a real fact that you are filled. Faith, however, perceives it as real fact that you are a Spirit-filled believer.** If you believe you are Spirit-filled, you believe you can speak and pray in tongues fluently. Because you believe that, you are going to act on that belief by endeavoring to pray in tongues daily, for the rest of your life if you have to, until you get a fluent tongue.

How do I know that this works? Because it worked for me; that's how I know.

CHAPTER 6

My Personal Testimony

I am living proof that any believer can be filled with the Holy Spirit, with the evidence of a fluent tongue. I am living proof that the baptism with the Holy Spirit is not merely an experience for "a select few" Christians, but for every Christian that believes. I am living proof that faith, when combined with patience, will lead every willing Christian into the infilling of the Holy Spirit, with supernatural evidence.

You see, I was the least likely candidate of any Christian to be filled with the Spirit. It wasn't that I was the worst sinner in the world growing up. As a matter of fact, I confessed Jesus as my Savior when I was about 12 years old. I did extremely well in school, and finished my senior year in high school with the highest grade point average. My class rank was No. 1. I made my parents proud. And for the most part, I stayed out of trouble.

What, then, was my problem? For one thing, my commitment to serving Jesus Christ as my Lord and Master was a shaky one, at best. I wasn't really living for God. I didn't do much Bible reading. I didn't pray much. I didn't go to church much. I didn't preach Christ to others (and didn't really understand that I was supposed to). And the Christian life, as a whole, was not real to me. (Can anyone identify with this? I know I'm not the only one who has been in this situation.) This casual, lukewarm approach to Christianity didn't exactly make me the No. 1 candidate to be filled with the Holy Spirit.

Fortunately, I had the privilege of being exposed to some committed, Bible-believing Christians in college who loved me, prayed for me, and helped to point me in the right direction. Even though I never fully accepted these Christians or their message while I was in college, they planted some good seeds in me and laid the groundwork for me to eventually recommit my life to the Lord in March of 1985.

But once I began to overcome the "lack of commitment" hurdle, the devil threw another obstacle in my path—and this one was seemingly insurmountable!

To make a long story short, I was exposed to a lie of the devil which just happens to be one of his favorites: "You can't make it to heaven because you've blasphemed the Holy Ghost!"

The devil has used this lie for years, and it has kept many sinners from receiving Christ. And I suspect it has kept many more Christians from making a strong commitment to the Christian life, in addition to being filled with the Holy Ghost. Satan likes to twist the scriptures for his own benefit, and this lie is partially based on scripture, but it's a lie nevertheless.

The Bible says the truth will set you free (John 8:32). There's no way in the world that you can set a person free by telling him that he has blasphemed the Holy Spirit and can't make it to heaven. Moreover, the Bible says that Jesus will never cast away from his presence anyone who sincerely comes to Him (John 6:37). And while it is true that the Bible does say that a person who blasphemes the Holy Spirit is not forgiven, the reason why the person is not forgiven, according to John 6:37, is because they never repent. Once you repent and sincerely come to God, according to 1 John 1:9, God not only forgives you of your sin but cleanses you from ALL unrighteousness! Not just some of it, but ALL of it! Hallelujah!

I am fully persuaded of these truths now. But at the time that the devil was challenging my faith in 1985, I was not fully persuaded of these things. I was not fully persuaded that if I came to Jesus in all sincerity, that he would accept me. I thought it was possible that Jesus would cast me away from his presence with an eternal death sentence. I wasn't fully persuaded that the devil was lying to me about the blasphemy of the Holy Ghost. I wasn't sure whether it was the devil or God who was speaking to me. I strongly suspected it was the devil, but I wasn't 100 percent sure. And so I lived for several months in mental torment, not being fully confident of my own salvation. What a horrible way to live!

To make a long story short, I came to the conclusion that I needed supernatural deliverance. By exposing myself to good, Bible-believing teachers, I learned that the baptism with the Holy Spirit is a supernatural experience which only believers can partake of. I knew in my heart that if I was filled with the Spirit with the evidence of speaking with other tongues, it would remove any doubts that I had about my own salvation. And so I began to pursue it.

In October 1987, I attended a crusade being held by my favorite Bible teacher in Washington, D.C. Before the close of the service, this minister extended some invitations, including an invitation to anyone who wanted to be filled with the Holy Spirit with the evidence of speaking with other tongues. I had never heard this invitation before, but I sensed in my spirit that I needed to respond to the invitation, so I did. A few hundred of us were escorted to a "lower room," where we were given instructions regarding salvation and the baptism with the Holy Spirit. Then they prayed with us to receive the Holy Spirit.

I would like to say that I immediately began to speak in a fluent tongue, but that would be lying. What really happened was that I opened my mouth and what came out sounded like . . . nothing. At its best, it sounded like unintelligible noise. It certainly didn't sound like a language. And all the while the devil was screaming in my ear. He said "You're not going to receive! You can't receive! You blasphemed the Holy

Ghost! You're going to hell! You're not even saved! Ha! Ha! Ha!" He kept yelling these things and repeating them. I tried to ignore him, but I admit I had a difficult time doing so. Especially because I had no fluent tongue.

I was confused and frustrated, but I hid it well.

At the request of the prayer room workers, we filled out some cards after the praying was completed. One of the questions was "Received the Holy Spirit? Yes or No." Our instructions were as follows: if we believed that we received the Holy Ghost, and believed that we were speaking in tongues *at least a little bit*, check Yes. The associate pastor also explained under what circumstances we were to check No. But he made it clear that if you checked No, you weren't checking No in faith. So, I thought about it and came to the conclusion that I had spoken in tongues *at least a little bit*. And responding with what little faith I had, I checked Yes.

Just to make sure I did it right, I asked a prayer room worker "Did I do this right?" He asked me if I had received the Holy Spirit. I thought about it a second, and said "I *believe* I have received the Holy Ghost." He smiled and said "Well, then, you checked it right!"

I smiled, thanked him, and walked away. I was still confused. I was still frustrated. I still didn't have a fluent tongue. All I had was just a glimmer of hope. A glimmer of faith. A glimmer of belief. Just a little faith, about the size of a mustard seed.

About nine months later, I found out where I missed it. After reading the book The Holy Spirit—The Missing Ingredient by Fred Price, I realized that there are times when it takes both faith AND perseverance to inherit the promises of God! I realized that there are situations where if you do not persevere, you will not be filled with the Holy Spirit with the evidence of a fluent tongue. And so I took a stand.

I remembered that I had checked Yes to the question "Received the Holy Ghost?" back in October of 1987. I decided it was time to act like I had received. I decided it was time to act like a Spirit-filled believer. I reasoned that since Spirit-filled believers speak in tongues, and I was Spirit-filled, that I could speak in tongues. **So I made a commitment before God that every day in my prayer time, FOR THE REST OF MY LIFE IF I HAD TO, I would not only pray in English, but that I would believe God to pray in tongues as well, UNTIL I RECEIVED A FLUENT TONGUE.**

Let me say it another way: by faith, I *perceived it as a real fact* that I was a Spirit-filled believer, even though it had *not yet been revealed to my senses*. Since I saw myself as being Spirit-filled, I acted like it. Since Spirit-filled believers pray in tongues, I prayed in tongues—that is, I spoke, and trusted the Holy Spirit to give me the words to say. I didn't care what it sounded like, because I knew in my heart that if I kept doing it, my faith would be rewarded.

About a week later (not seven years later, not seven months later, but a *week* later), it happened. I was lying in bed worshipping God, but not speaking a word of English, just trusting the Holy Spirit to give me the words to say. The next thing I knew, it seemed like rivers of living water were pouring out of my mouth! I didn't really feel anything, but a supernatural language began to flow out of me. As I kept praying, it sounded beautiful to my ears. It wasn't English, but I knew it was a language. The devil began to yell "You're not filled! You're not filled!" But it was too late. I knew in my heart that I was filled. **I had *received* back in October of 1987, but I was *filled* in July of 1988. Hallelujah!**

I was ecstatic. I began weeping for joy. The devil could no longer torment me with the lie that I had blasphemed the Holy Ghost. I knew what the Bible said about the outward evidence of the baptism with the Holy Spirit. I knew that the Holy Spirit baptism was only for believers. And my speaking in tongues confirmed what I had already believed deep down in my heart but had doubted in my head—that I was indeed saved. Glory to God!

I said all of that to say this: **if a believer who is being tormented by the devil about the blasphemy of the Holy Spirit can be filled with the Spirit with the evidence of a fluent tongue, then who can't be filled?**

I said it earlier in the chapter, and I'll say it again: **faith, when combined with patience (or perseverance), will lead**

every willing Christian into the infilling of the Holy Spirit, with supernatural evidence.

As you can see, I have a very good reason for believing that there is a difference between receiving the Holy Spirit and being filled with the Holy Spirit. **I know there is a difference based on my own experience. My own testimony proves it out.** *And I know in my heart that those of you who are chronic seekers of the Holy Spirit will be set free if you believe what I'm sharing with you and you act on it.*

But it isn't just my testimony. **The Word of God also proves it out,** simply by using different words with different meanings (receive, fill, baptize) to describe different aspects of the same event.

No matter how you look at it, there is hope for the Christian who believes he has received the Holy Spirit, but has no discernible "tongue" to show for it. Add perseverance to your faith. Commit yourself to praying in tongues in your everyday prayer life. Speak, and trust the Holy Spirit to give you the words to say. The Holy Spirit will do His part. He will give you the words to say in a language which is unfamiliar to your natural mind. Supernatural words and supernatural prayers are in the depths of your spirit, just waiting for the opportunity to come out. Just trust Him (never stop trusting Him) and speak out.

CHAPTER 7

Why Speak in Tongues?

By now, I hope that I have made it clear that the baptism with the Holy Spirit, with the evidence of speaking in tongues, is available to every believer. This doesn't mean that every believer is necessarily going to speak in tongues. But it does mean that every believer has the ability to speak in tongues, as the result of being filled with the Spirit.

"And these signs shall follow THEM THAT BELIEVE; in my name shall they cast out devils; they shall SPEAK WITH NEW TONGUES"(Mark 16:17).

In other words, to those who believe in Jesus with a simple, uncomplicated, unrestricted, unlimited faith, these signs will follow them. One of these signs is speaking with new tongues as the result of being filled with the Spirit.

Some people are filled with the Spirit immediately after salvation, and they receive the supernatural manifestation of tongues immediately. Others have to exercise their faith for it. Others have to combine faith with perseverance in order to see the manifestation of speaking in tongues, as I noted with my personal testimony in the last chapter. **But regardless of how it happens, the baptism with the Holy**

Spirit is available to every believer. Every believer can speak in tongues.

Well, if that's true, why doesn't every believer speak in tongues?

There are several reasons. In some cases, Christians don't speak in tongues because they *do not follow the instructions given to them* when a pastor or minister is praying for them to receive. We will discuss this more in the next few chapters, when we talk about how to receive.

But in this chapter, I want to focus on another reason why many believers do not speak in tongues—lack of hunger. The Bible says that those who hunger and thirst after righteousness shall be filled (Matthew 5:6). Many Christians, for one reason or another, do not hunger for more of God. Many Christians do not hunger for the baptism with the Holy Spirit. *And one reason why many Christians do not hunger or thirst for the baptism with the Holy Spirit is that they do not understand the purpose of the experience, nor do they understand the purpose of tongues.*

Because they don't understand the purpose of tongues, they shy away from the Holy Ghost baptism entirely. Or in some cases, they do receive the Holy Ghost without getting a fluent tongue, and instead of sticking it out, they quit. *If you don't understand the purpose of a thing, it is highly unlikely that you will persevere until you get it.*

Why should every believer speak in tongues? The

reasons are numerous, but let me just name a few.

1. Tongues are the initial outward sign that you have been filled with the Holy Spirit. You don't have to wait till you get to heaven to find out if you are filled with the Holy Spirit or not. You can know that right now. Not just by faith, but by supernatural evidence.

2. Tongues can provide added assurance of your own salvation. When I say "tongues" here, I am speaking of a fluent tongue.

Notice that I didn't say that speaking in tongues proves that you are saved. Anyone who is saved knows it deep down in his or her heart, or spirit—regardless of whether or not you speak in tongues. But what many people do not realize is that mankind is a threefold being—spirit, soul, and body (I Thessalonians 5:23). And the Word of God makes a distinction between the spirit and soul (Hebrews 4:12). The spirit is the "real you," and the soul consists of your mind, emotions, will, and intellect. So it is possible to know something in your spirit, but to have all kinds of doubt about it in your mind (which is part of the soul). *And since many Christians are mind-ruled instead of spirit-ruled, you have a lot of Christians today who aren't sure about their own salvation.* Deep down, they sense that they really are saved, but their mind is so confused, they honestly don't know what to think.

Speaking in tongues, when combined with knowledge of the Word of God, can provide added assurance of your own salvation. The Word of God says that the world cannot receive the Holy Ghost, meaning that only believers can (John 14:16-17). If that's true, then you are no exception to the rule. If you are filled with the Holy Spirit, according to the Bible you are a believer. You are saved from hell. Isn't that great! Hallelujah!

This may come as a surprise to some of you, but God wants you to know that you are saved! Psalm 107:2 states "Let the redeemed of the Lord SAY SO." How can they say it if they don't know they are redeemed? How can <u>you</u> say it if <u>you</u> don't know you are redeemed? Think about it. To redeem means "to buy back." In this case, it means "to buy back from the hand of the enemy." In effect, it means you have been saved from the enemy! The Bible says you are supposed to SAY that you have been bought back, or saved, from the hand of the enemy. In order to say it, you must first of all *know* it.

Moreover, 1 John 5:13 says very plainly that you are supposed to know that you have eternal life. There is no guesswork involved; you are supposed to *know*. Anything that provides you with added assurance of your own salvation is a good thing. Tongues are a good thing. Don't fight them. Don't try to reason them away. Don't try to make excuses why you can't speak in tongues. Don't try to make excuses why you can't be filled. Just believe and receive!

3. Tongues are a means of building yourself up spiritually. 1 Corinthians 14:4 says "He that speaketh in an unknown tongue edifieth himself." To edify yourself means to build yourself up. When you speak in an unknown tongue, you are speaking divine secrets unto God (1 Cor. 14:2). Even though you don't understand the language that you are speaking, God does. It is a supernatural means of communication with God, and it builds you up spiritually.

Not only can you speak to God in tongues, but you can speak to yourself in tongues! (See 1 Cor. 14:28). And you should! Speaking in tongues refreshes the spirit man (Isaiah 28:11,12). Not only that, but it provides a means of protection against the negative influences and pressures of the world. If you are at work, for example, and all your co-workers are swearing and telling dirty jokes, you can "stay clean" by speaking and praying in tongues under your breath, building yourself up in your spirit man.

4. Tongues are a reminder that the Holy Spirit is living on the inside of you. Remember the example in Chapter 5 about the glass of water receiving water, being filled with water, and being baptized with water? Remember also that I mentioned about an Alka-Seltzer tablet being put in the glass, but I never explained the significance of that tablet.

The tablet represents the Holy Spirit, who lives in the heart of every believer, regardless of whether a person speaks in tongues or not. But when the water hits that tablet, something happens! Power is released! And that is symbolic of a person being filled to overflowing with the Holy Spirit, with the initial evidence of speaking in tongues. "But ye shall receive POWER, after that the Holy Ghost is come upon you" (Acts 1:8). This is the "divine ability" that I spoke of in Chapter 1. The Holy Spirit is a Strengthener, because he adds divine ability to your natural ability.

Any time a Spirit-filled believer speaks in tongues, it reminds him that the Holy Ghost is living on the inside of him. Now, it is possible to speak in tongues mindlessly, without thinking about what you are doing. But I'm not talking about that. What I am saying is this: any time a Spirit-filled believer prays in tongues, it is a reminder to him that the Holy Ghost is living in him. After all, you couldn't pray that way without the Holy Ghost inside you giving you the supernatural words to say. So every time you do it, it is a reminder: the Holy Ghost is living in me. God is living in me! God is dwelling in me!

Once you realize that God is living and dwelling in you, the desire to sin leaves! The desire to please God increases! Praise the Lord! So obviously, the more you pray and speak in tongues, the more of an awareness you have that the Holy Ghost is living on the inside of you, and the less you are going to sin! The more you pray and speak in tongues, the more you are going to live a righteous and holy lifestyle. After all, if Jesus Christ were staying at your house for two weeks, how often would you sin? Not much, I'm sure.

I'm talking about Holy Ghost power here! Divine ability. And this ability, when used in prayer and meditation, is a powerful source of strength to the believer. This power can be used to defeat alcoholism, drug and cigarette addiction, sexual addiction, and other sins of the flesh.

Allow me to use a rather blunt example to illustrate the point (for mature audiences only). If you are squeamish about the subject of sex, perhaps you should skip this part. But I wouldn't do that if I were you. The truth will set you free!

Let's say a man is having trouble controlling himself sexually. He has a strong lust for the opposite sex, and he acts out that lust through masturbation. Then he receives Jesus as His Saviour, but still has problems with lust and masturbation. But then he is filled with the Spirit, with the Bible evidence of speaking with other tongues. The same desires come into his mind, but this time the man is Spirit-filled. Every time the lustful thoughts begin to enter his mind, he begins to pray in a fluent tongue, sending a supernatural reminder to his brain that the Holy Spirit is living on the inside of him. As a result, those desires leave! Every time the desires come, he begins to praise the Lord in tongues, and the desires leave! And so, where this man used to struggle to resist lust, now there is virtually no struggle at all—provided, of course, that he chooses to activate that "divine ability" on the inside of him.

Hey, there's no sense in me lying about it. I speak from experience.

When I was still single, and was tempted to lust after women and to act on that lust, I put these principles into practice, and they worked wonders for me. I would praise the Lord in tongues, and it reminded me that I had the Holy Spirit living in me. It gave me a wonderful sense of self-control that I had never thought was possible. Yes, men can resist temptation! Yes, men don't have to give in to the lusts of the flesh! And the same applies to women as well! But I say again, the supernatural power to combat these lusts comes through the baptism with the Holy Spirit, with the Bible evidence of speaking with other tongues.

This is why it is so important that you have a fluent tongue. If your tongue is not fluent, it is not going to remind you that the Holy Spirit is living on the inside of you, because the devil will tell you, "Oh, it's just you doing that. God isn't giving you the utterance." If your tongue isn't fluent, you will be likely to believe the devil. And you aren't going to be convinced that the Holy Spirit is living on the inside of you. And you are going to sin more, and have a lot more trouble living a righteous and holy lifestyle. Some of you are at this place in your lives right now! But you can be set free before you finish reading this book, praise God!

What about all those Spirit-filled believers who are living an *unrighteous* lifestyle? Remind me to discuss that topic before the end of this book. (See the Appendix, which has a Question and Answer section.)

5. Tongues stimulate faith. Jude 20 reads as follows: "…Building up yourselves on your most holy FAITH, praying in the Holy Ghost." Praying in tongues stimulates faith and helps us learn how to develop trust in God. After all, when you pray in tongues, you have no idea what you are going to say next. You are dependent upon the Holy Spirit to give you the words to say. That takes faith.

Why is that important? Well, the Bible says the just are supposed to live by faith. The Bible says this is the victory that overcomes the world, even our faith. The Bible says you cannot please God without faith (Hebrews 11:6). Enough said.

6. Tongues help your prayer life. They help you to pray in line with God's perfect will and to pray for the unknown. Romans 8:26 says "…We know not what we should pray for as we ought, but the Spirit itself maketh intercession for us with groanings which cannot be uttered." Have you ever tried to pray for someone or something in English, but you didn't really know what you should pray for? Praying in tongues helps in this case, because when you pray in tongues, you are praying the perfect will of God over the situation.

Moreover, we can be supernaturally led by the Holy Spirit to pray in tongues about a situation which our natural mind knows nothing about. For example, you might be led to pray in tongues for an hour and not know why. Later, you find out that your mother was in an automobile accident, but she wasn't hurt at all, and the car only suffered minor damage. The accident occurred at the time you were praying. If you hadn't obeyed the Holy Ghost and prayed, your mother may have suffered a worse fate. Thank God for the Holy Ghost!

7. Tongues are a means of giving thanks. According to I Corinthians 14:17, a person who prays in tongues "giveth thanks well." So praying in tongues can be a supernatural means of giving thanks to God. We should give thanks to God both in English (with our minds) and in tongues (with our spirits).

8. Tongues are a means of keeping your tongue in check. Of all the parts of your body, the tongue is the most difficult to control. "For the tongue can no man tame; it is an unruly evil, full of deadly poison" (James 3:8). All of us have at times said the wrong thing at the wrong time. We have offended others, or we have spoken negative thoughts about ourselves or others. In our own power, there isn't much we can do to stop this from happening. But with God, all things are possible.

When we receive Jesus as our Lord, we are yielding ourselves to Him. We are yielding every part of our beings to Him. Or at least we *should* be doing so. And that should include yielding our tongues to Him. If we can yield our tongues to Him by yielding our tongues to the Holy Spirit, it is a big step toward yielding everything to Him.

When you speak in tongues or pray in tongues, you are yielding your tongue to the Holy Spirit. You are allowing the Holy Spirit to give you the words to say, so you can say what He wants you to say rather than what you want to say. This is why people who are bound by pride have trouble receiving the Holy Spirit. They don't want to yield their tongue to anyone but themselves. They want the right to say what they want to say, and they will fight for that right! Consequently, yielding their tongues to the Holy Spirit is a struggle for them.

If that is a good description of yourself, I encourage you to repent right now. Humble yourself before the Lord, confess your sin, and turn from it. Receive the Holy Spirit and be filled!

CHAPTER 8

The Will of God

In the first edition of this book, Chapter 8 was entitled How to Receive. That chapter is also included in this edition of the book, but it has been moved to Chapter 10. Some of you may be so ready to receive the Holy Ghost, you might be able to skip Chapters 8 and 9, go right to Chapter 10, and receive the Holy Spirit right away with the evidence of speaking in tongues, praise God! If you do this, no problem; I won't be offended.

Having said that, I want to do my part to ensure that, regardless of your religious background (or non-religious background), those of you who want to receive the Holy Spirit actually do receive, and that you also have the supernatural evidence that the Bible says you are supposed to have. For that reason, I have added two more chapters that were not in the first edition.

By now you have probably already figured out that I believe it is the will of God that every born-again believer be filled with the Holy Spirit, speaking in tongues. And many of you may accept that conclusion with no problems whatsoever. If so, you can probably skip the next two chapters. But different people come from different religious backgrounds, and I realize that some of you may not agree about the will of

God on this matter. To those of you who are not persuaded yet, this chapter is for you. (And the next one is, too.)

But I want to remind you of something I said in the Introduction—you need to desire the truth about tongues and the baptism with the Holy Spirit *regardless of whether it lines up with your preexisting beliefs.* If that desire for the truth is not there, nothing that I say is going to persuade you to change your existing beliefs, and you might as well put this book down and do something else. But if that desire is there, I encourage you to hang tight and keep reading. I intend to make a scriptural case that the baptism with the Holy Spirit is the will of God for every believer.

First, it is a given that Jesus dedicated himself to doing the will of God when he was on the earth. He said he came not to do his own will, but the will of the Father who sent him (John 6:38). So if Jesus did it, it was the will of God. If Jesus said it, then it was the will of God.

So what did Jesus say regarding speaking in tongues?

And these signs shall follow those who believe. . .THEY WILL SPEAK WITH NEW TONGUES. . . . - Mark 16:17

I don't see any ambiguity in what Jesus is saying here. He is making it plain. Those who believe will speak with tongues.

As I said earlier, this doesn't mean that every believer is necessarily going to speak in tongues. To make such a statement doesn't line up with reality. But let's not water down what Jesus said here to the point that it doesn't mean anything. At minimum, it means that every believer has the ability to speak in tongues, as the result of being filled with the Spirit. What else could it mean?

I'm sure some of you who disagree and like to argue might be able to come up with an alternative explanation of what Jesus meant here. But it's not enough to just come up with an alternative explanation. You need an alternative explanation that lines up with the rest of the scriptures. And that is impossible to do with any reliability, unless you do so by revelation of the Spirit of God. And the Spirit of God will always lead us (and reveal things to us) in line with the Word of God. And the Word of God plainly indicates that those who believe can speak with tongues.

Look, if Jesus said it, it is the will of God.

Speaking in tongues is the will of God for believers. It is not the will of God in the sense that every believer will actually do it. But it is the perfect will of God for Christians; it is what God desires to see in the lives of ALL believers.

God's will is revealed in His Word. His Word says that those who believe can speak with tongues. God's Word also says "Be filled with the Spirit" (Eph. 5:18).

That pretty much settles it as far as God's will is concerned. We've already established that when the Bible refers to being "filled with the Spirit," it generally is referring to the baptism with the Holy Spirit, which includes speaking in tongues.

Why am I spending so much time on this? Because this is an area where many Christians miss it. They have doubts regarding whether it is the will of God for them to be filled with the Holy Spirit and speak with tongues. Now faith will work in your heart, even with doubt in your head. But as long as you are entertaining those doubts, and giving them serious consideration, receiving the Holy Spirit will be more of a challenge to you than it really should be.

Speaking of "receiving the Holy Spirit," I want to make a very important point here. *It isn't up to God to give you the Holy Spirit. It's up to you to receive the Holy Spirit.* It was the will of God for the Holy Spirit to be given to the church on the day of Pentecost, and the Holy Spirit has been here ever since. He never left. So the process of God giving the Holy Spirit has already occurred. It is now a matter of you receiving, rather than God giving.

Some of you may have a hard time wrapping your head around that, particularly if you come from a religious background that gives God the credit (or blame) for doing everything. But if you truly study what the Bible has to say, from Genesis to Revelation, you will find out that in most cases, there is a "God side" and a "man side" to everything. This is true of salvation, for example. God so loved the world, that He gave Jesus as a sacrifice for mankind (John 3:16). That was the "God side"; God made the first move. But in order for us to receive the benefit of what Jesus did, we must confess with our mouth the Lord Jesus and believe in our hearts that God raised Jesus from the dead (Romans 10:9). That is the "man side." So salvation has a "God side" and a "man side," and the same is true of healing. And the same is true of the baptism with the Holy Spirit.

And whether you are talking about salvation, or healing, or the baptism with the Holy Spirit, they all have one thing in common—*God has already done His part.* In other words, the "God side" is already taken care of. It was the will of God that the Holy Spirit be poured out on the Day of Pentecost. He is already here. God did his part.

Now it is up to us. We must believe and receive.

Jesus promised us that if we believe, we can expect supernatural signs, including speaking in tongues. Now Jesus wasn't trying to say that it would happen automatically, because as a rule, it won't. But he did say that these signs would follow "them that believe." So if you are Christian, and you believe that this supernatural sign will follow you, and you expect it, and you act on it (by speaking in faith and trusting the Holy Spirit to give you the supernatural words to say), it will happen.

The baptism with the Holy Spirit is a promise of God to believers. We can bank on it.

CHAPTER 9

The Promise of the Father

In the last chapter, we established that speaking in tongues is the will of God for every believer. I want to further establish this truth in this chapter by looking at what the Word of God has to say about "the promise of the Father."

In Luke 24:49, after Christ's resurrection, Jesus told the disciples that he would send "the promise of my Father." But he told them to tarry (or wait) in Jerusalem, until they were "endued with power from on high."

In Acts 1:4-5, Jesus is quoted as telling the disciples essentially the same thing. He said they should not depart from Jerusalem, but "wait for the PROMISE OF THE FATHER. . .For John truly baptized with water, but YOU SHALL BE BAPTIZED WITH THE HOLY SPIRIT not many days from now." Note that Jesus refers to the baptism with the Holy Spirit as "the promise of the Father."

Jesus' last words before ascending to heaven included the following:

But YOU SHALL RECEIVE POWER WHEN THE HOLY SPIRIT HAS COME UPON YOU; and you shall be witnesses to Me in Jerusalem, and in all Judea and Samaria, and to the end of the earth. – Acts 1:8

And these signs shall follow those who believe … THEY WILL SPEAK WITH NEW TONGUES… - Mark 16:17

It should be pretty obvious from these scriptures that Jesus, at minimum, wanted his disciples to be filled with the Holy Spirit, with the evidence of speaking in tongues.

In Acts 2, his disciples were filled with the Spirit, and indeed they spoke with tongues, just as Jesus promised! Hallelujah!

"Well, that is wonderful," you may say. "Jesus' disciples were filled with the Spirit 2,000 years ago and spoke with tongues. Good for them! But that doesn't mean that it is for us today. That was just for the early church."

I see a few problems with this way of thinking:

For one thing, Jesus never said it was only for the disciples of the early church. As I pointed out in the last chapter, Jesus made it clear that the sign of speaking in tongues would not just follow the early church disciples, but would follow "those who believe" (Mark 16:17).

If there were any doubt whatsoever about whether speaking in tongues is for believers today, Peter ended all doubt with his comments in Acts 2.

Therefore being exalted to the right hand of God, and having received from the Father the PROMISE OF THE HOLY SPIRIT, He poured out THIS WHICH YOU NOW SEE AND HEAR. . . .Repent, and let every one of you be baptized in the name of Jesus Christ for the remission of sins; and you shall receive the GIFT OF THE HOLY SPIRIT. For the PROMISE IS TO YOU and to YOUR CHILDREN, and to ALL WHO ARE AFAR OFF, AS MANY AS THE LORD OUR GOD WILL CALL. – Acts 2:33, 38-39

Peter's statement has great significance. For one thing, he equates the "promise of the Holy Spirit" with "this which you now see and hear," so we know he is talking about the baptism with the Holy Spirit and speaking in tongues. Secondly, Peter also refers to the Holy Spirit as a gift, equating the baptism with the Holy Spirit to receiving the "gift of the Holy Spirit." And thirdly, he makes it clear who this "gift" and "promise" of the Holy Spirit is for. It was for the disciples in the early church, yes. But it was also for their children. It was also for "all who were afar off."

And it is also to "as many as the Lord our God will call." Praise the Lord!

This includes all Christians. I see no Christians left out here.

Remember that Jesus said "if I be lifted up from the earth, I will draw all men unto me" (John 12:32). This does not mean that all men (including unsaved men) are supposed to speak in tongues. Remember that Jesus said these signs should follow "those who believe." But by saying "as many as the Lord our God will call," it implies at minimum that ALL believers—ALL who have answered God's call to salvation by receiving Jesus as Lord and Master—are eligible to receive this gift.

So that settles it. The promise of the Holy Spirit is for ALL believers. No exceptions.

Moreover, 2 Corinthians 1:20 states that ALL of the promises of God in Christ are "yes" and "amen." The word "no" is not included in that verse. Do you understand the significance of that? That means God doesn't say "no," at least not where his promises are concerned. When it comes to the promises of God that were fulfilled in Christ, God only responds with "yes" and "amen." In other words, "yes" and "yes." Hallelujah!

This does not mean that every believer will receive the Holy Spirit, and speak in tongues. But they should. And they can. Yes and yes. And if you are a believer, and you haven't received yet, you should. And the good news is, you can. Yes. you can!

If you are a believer in Jesus Christ, you can speak in tongues. And it isn't hard. At least it doesn't have to be.

Are you ready? If so, the next chapter gives details on how to receive. Prepare to be Spirit-filled!

CHAPTER 10

How Do I Receive?

In the last chapter, we discussed why tongues are so important. In this chapter, we will discuss the "how" of tongues—as in "How Do I Receive?"

What you must understand first is that you don't need to meet an eight-step qualification process in order to be eligible to receive the Holy Spirit. The only basic requirement that you need to meet is to be saved. According to John 14:17, the world (unsaved people) cannot receive the Holy Ghost. This means that only believers can receive. Only the saved.

How do you know you are saved? If you have done what the Bible says regarding salvation, you are saved. In other words, if you have confessed with your mouth Jesus as your Master and Saviour, and you believe in your heart that God has raised Jesus from the dead, you are saved (Romans 10:9).

I know that sounds too simple to be true, but it is! Salvation is a simple process. But I don't want to oversimplify it. If you truly are confessing Jesus as your Saviour and Master, that means that you are turning away from your previous Master, the devil.

"What? The devil is my master?" Yes, if you are an unsaved person, the devil is your master, whether you realize it or not. It is the devil who tells people "Hey, do what you want to do! Live how you want to live! Be your own Master!" So, if you choose to be your own Master, instead of allowing Jesus to be your Master, then in reality you are allowing the devil to be your Master. As one song aptly put it, you gotta serve somebody. Either you are serving the Lord Jesus, or you are serving the devil. Period.

The earth belongs to the Lord, but the world system that we live in currently belongs to the devil (2 Cor. 4:4), and that has been the case since the fall of Adam. Adam formerly had dominion over this world (Genesis 1:26), but he sinned and turned over that dominion to the devil (Luke 4:5-6). Now the devil's lease on this world system is a limited one, but he still has power and influence over this world. He works night and day in an attempt to deceive, steal from, kill, and destroy mankind. He is destined to burn in the lake of fire, but he wants to take a lot of people with him. The only way to break his power over your life is to invite Jesus Christ to come into your heart and life, and to allow Jesus to rule your life.

If you have never received Jesus Christ as your personal Saviour and Master, and you would like to do so right now, I encourage you to pray the following prayer:

Father, I come before you right now in the name of your precious son, the Lord Jesus Christ. Father, I realize

that I am a sinner, that I am lost without Jesus Christ in my heart. I realize that I am bound for hell unless I receive Jesus as my Saviour. And so I do that right now. According to Romans 10:9, if I confess with my mouth Jesus as my Master, and I believe in my heart that you raised Jesus from the dead, I will be saved. Your Word is true, and I know you cannot lie. So I confess Jesus right now as my Master. I say that the devil is no longer my master. I say that Jesus Christ is my Master, as well as my Saviour. From this day forward, I plan to allow Jesus Christ to rule my life, and I ask Jesus to come into my heart right now. Cleanse me from my sins and make me a new creature. I invite Jesus Christ into my spirit, so that my life can be transformed and that you may be glorified. I ask this in Jesus' name. Amen.

If you prayed that prayer in all sincerity, you are now saved! Praise the Lord! And you are ready right now to receive the Holy Spirit!

Remember, Jesus Christ is now your Master. And Jesus said "You shall receive power, after the Holy Ghost is come upon you" (Acts 1:8). It was Jesus that said "For these signs shall follow them that believe…they shall speak with new tongues" (Mark 16:17). It is clear from these passages that it is the will of God and of his son Jesus that you be filled with the Holy Spirit, with the Bible evidence of speaking with other tongues.

Let's not make this any harder than it is. If the Head of the Church wants you to receive the Holy Spirit, it must be a pretty good idea. So if you've been fighting this, don't fight it anymore. Jesus is your Master now. Receive!

Some of you are ready right now, so I will offer you instructions on how to receive. Read over the following prayer, and make sure you have a basic understanding of what the prayer is asking for. Then pray this prayer out loud and prepare your heart to receive the Holy Spirit!

Father, I thank you for saving me from hell. I thank you for your Son, the Lord Jesus Christ. I thank you for the Spirit of Christ that now resides in my heart. And Father, I now realize that in addition to my salvation, it is your desire that I be filled to overflowing with the Holy Spirit; that I be filled to overflowing with divine power. Father, I want that divine power. Father, I want that divine ability. I know that I cannot live the kind of life that you want me to live without the infilling of the Holy Spirit. And so right now I purpose in my heart to receive the Holy Spirit, to be filled to overflowing with the Holy Ghost. Holy Spirit, come into my spirit right now, and fill me to overflowing with your presence. I thank you in advance. In Jesus name I pray. Amen.

Now, you are ready to receive. Receive in Jesus name! Then yield your tongue to the Holy Spirit and speak!

CHAPTER 11

Where Did I Miss It?

Praise the Lord! I am thankful that some of you who prayed the prayer to receive the Holy Spirit have already been filled to overflowing with the Holy Spirit, with the evidence of speaking in a fluent tongue. Some of you, I am certain, started speaking in tongues even before you finished praying! Praise God that it is possible for some people to be filled without praying at all!

But I am also certain that there are a number of people reading this book who still are not seeing the manifestation of a fluent tongue even after they have prayed. If you are one of those people, this chapter is for you.

Before we go any further, you must understand two things:

1. God never fails. So if you are not speaking in a fluent tongue, it isn't God's fault. Don't blame God. Don't think that just because you didn't see the manifestation, that it must not be the will of God for you to be filled with the Spirit. God's will is revealed in His Word, and His Word says "Be filled with the Spirit" (Eph. 5:18). That pretty much settles it as far as God's will is concerned.

2. It isn't up to God to give you the Holy Spirit. It's up to you to receive the Holy Spirit. To reiterate a point made in

Chapter 8, God gave the Holy Spirit to the church on the day of Pentecost, and the Holy Spirit has been here ever since. The process of God giving the Holy Spirit has already occurred. It is now a matter of you receiving, rather than God giving.

Unless you humble yourself and are willing to accept these points, becoming filled with the Holy Spirit will continue to be difficult for you.

Having said that, let's discuss some of the main areas where people tend to miss it when it comes to receiving the Holy Spirit. Then we will discuss how to receive again, and those who didn't experience a fluent tongue the first time will be better prepared this time.

1. Being filled with the Holy Spirit is NOT the same thing as speaking in tongues. This point is a stumbling block for many people. They think that speaking in tongues is the same thing as being filled with the Holy Spirit. And so they actually try to speak in tongues without having first been filled with the Spirit. They may pray a prayer to receive the Holy Spirit, but their mind really isn't on receiving the Third Person of the Godhead in His fullness. Their mind is on the tongues. "Will I be able to speak in tongues, or not?" They get hung up on the tongues, and as a result, they don't do the one thing that is absolutely necessary to see the manifestation of the tongues—receiving the Holy Spirit.

Friend, the baptism with the Holy Spirit is not the same thing as speaking with tongues. They are related, but they are not the same thing. Speaking in tongues is a natural consequence of being filled to overflowing with the Holy Spirit. If you are filled to overflowing with the Holy Ghost, speaking in tongues will be the very next thing that happens. And you won't have to make it happen. You *do* have to *cooperate* with the Holy Spirit, but you don't have to make it happen. If you yield to the Holy Spirit, and allow Him to fill you with His presence, you won't have to worry about the tongues. They will happen.

Let me explain it another way. Water is wet. Anytime you find water in its natural state, it is wet. Wet is a natural byproduct of having water. So water and wet are related. But that doesn't mean they are the same thing. That said, if you want to experience the wetness that comes from water, you must first of all have the water.

In similar fashion, the infilling of the Holy Spirit results in the act of speaking with other tongues. Anytime a person is filled to overflowing with the Spirit, they speak with tongues. So being filled with the Spirit and speaking in tongues are related. But they are not the same thing. However, if you want to experience the tongues that come as a byproduct of having been filled with the Holy Spirit, you must first of all receive the Holy Spirit.

What am I saying? I'm saying that tongues shouldn't be your primary focus. Receiving the Holy Spirit should be your primary focus. Being filled to overflowing with the Holy Spirit should be your primary focus. Tongues is only the *initial* outward evidence that you have been filled. It is not the only outward evidence. Prophecy (supernatural utterance in a *known* tongue) is also evidence that you have been filled with the Spirit (Acts 19:6). Speaking supernaturally to yourselves in psalms, hymns, and spiritual songs is also evidence that you have been filled with the Spirit (Ephesians 5:18-19). It isn't just about tongues. Receiving the Holy Spirit is more important than merely speaking in tongues.

So don't try to speak in tongues first. RECEIVE first. Then yield your tongue to the Holy Spirit and speak.

2. It isn't the Holy Spirit who does the speaking. *You do.* I mentioned earlier that many Christians have trouble with the infilling of the Spirit because they do not follow the instructions given to them. For example, their pastor will explain to them: "It isn't the Holy Spirit who does the speaking. <u>You</u> do." But when it comes time for them to speak in tongues, instead of speaking, they wait. Wait for what? They wait for the <u>Holy Spirit</u> to speak. While that may *seem* like the right thing to do, it actually is a hindrance to the process of becoming filled with the Spirit.

I was working as an usher in a church a few years ago when a pastor was praying with a young lady to be filled with the Spirit. As the pastor gave this lady instructions, he made it clear that the Holy Spirit would do His part by empowering her to speak, but that <u>she</u> would have to do the speaking.

His instructions were very good. But when the time came to receive the Holy Spirit, this young lady would not open her mouth. She just stood there with eyes closed, hands raised, and mouth closed. The pastor tried to get her to cooperate with the Holy Spirit by opening her mouth, but she refused to do so. Needless to say, she was not filled with the Spirit.

I tried to find her after the service to talk with her and encourage her, but I never found her. And to my dismay, I never saw her set foot in that church again.

What happened? Obviously this lady was waiting for the Holy Spirit to do the speaking for her. She thought if she just stood there with her mouth shut, the Holy Spirit would just grab her tongue and make her speak. If you believe the same thing she did, I have a word for you: **Wrong!**

Speaking in tongues is a cooperative effort between you and the Holy Spirit. The Holy Spirit provides the words to speak, but <u>you</u> speak them.

I want to spend a little time on this one, because a large number of people who have trouble speaking in tongues miss it in this area. They think that because the Holy Spirit is involved, the Holy Spirit will speak in tongues for them. They think that the Holy Spirit will speak <u>through</u> them. They think that the Holy Spirit will do all the work, and that they don't actually have to do anything. All of these ideas are either wrong or misleading.

Acts 2:4 says "And <u>they</u> were all filled with the Holy

Ghost, and began to speak in other tongues..." <u>They</u> spoke. The subject of Acts 2:4 is "they." "They" began to speak. Not the Holy Ghost. "They" began to speak. The Holy Ghost gave them the words to say, but *they* spoke the words. The Holy Ghost doesn't speak in tongues. <u>You</u> do.

For some of you that are still confused, let me offer this illustration:

The President of the United States normally has a press secretary who is responsible for releasing information to the press. This person also may have some input into what the President will say at a given press conference. In fact, in some cases, the President will not speak on his own; he may read a text prepared for him by the press secretary. In cases like this, the President speaks *as the press secretary gives him the words to say, or as the press secretary gives him utterance.*

Similarly, when you speak in tongues, you (the President) speak as the Holy Spirit (the press secretary) gives you the utterance!

Notice in the above example that even though it was the press secretary who prepared the words for the President to speak, it was the <u>President</u> who actually spoke those words out, not the press secretary. Similarly, even though the Holy Spirit is the one who gives you the utterance, you are the one who has to speak in tongues, not the Holy Spirit. You are the agent who is primarily responsible for making sure that the supernatural words given to you by the Holy Spirit come up out of your belly and out of your mouth. **And if you don't do it, you have no Biblical assurance that it will happen.** You see, the Bible pattern is that *we* speak as the Holy Spirit gives us the words to say. *We* speak in tongues.

Nowhere in the Bible does it ever say the Holy Spirit speaks in tongues. That's not his job. His job is to help *you* do it. (That's one reason He is called the Helper). And without his help, you couldn't speak in tongues. With his help, you can do it. But your job is to allow the Holy Spirit to *help* you speak, rather than expect the Holy Spirit to speak *for* you. There's a big difference. And if you don't see the difference, let me further illustrate it in a way that will bring it home for you.

Let's say I invite you over to my house to *help* me do the dishes. You say, "How can I help? Do you want me to wash, or dry?" I say "Both. I want you to wash and dry, while I watch TV." By this time, you may suspect that I didn't really invite you over to my house to *help* me do the dishes, but to have you do the dishes *for* me. And you would probably object, and rightfully so. In similar fashion, the Holy Spirit is ever present to *help* you speak in tongues, but not to speak in tongues *for* you. The Holy Spirit certainly has his part, but don't neglect your responsibility when it comes to speaking in tongues. *You* speak.

3. Lack of hunger (or thirst) is a hindrance to being filled with the Spirit.

"If any man thirst, let him come unto me and drink.

"He that believeth on me, as the scripture hath said, *out of his belly shall flow rivers of living water*" (John 7:37-38).

I won't spend much time on this one, because it was already covered in the beginning of Chapter 7, "Why Speak in Tongues." If you suspect that this may be your problem, you would do well to reread that chapter. In the meantime, remember this: *if you are not hungry or thirsty for something, it is highly unlikely that you will persevere until you get it.* Understanding the benefits of tongues, combined with humbling yourself and realizing that you need more of God, should increase your hunger and thirst level for the baptism with the Holy Spirit. And speaking of humbling yourself...

4. Pride is a hindrance to being filled with the Spirit. "...God *resisteth* the proud, but giveth grace to the humble" (James 4:6).

Pride takes you out of position to receive the Holy Spirit in his fullness. A prideful person says "I'll receive the Holy Spirit on my terms, not God's. I want the Holy Spirit, but not the tongues." Or such a person will receive the Holy Spirit, but will only speak in tongues under his breath, not loud enough for anyone to hear. Why? Because the person is afraid that his tongue may not be fluent, and is afraid of what people might think as a result. "Maybe they won't think I'm spiritual! Maybe they won't look up to me like they once did."

That may seem innocent enough to you, but when you finally break it all down, it's pride.

A prideful person only thinks of himself (or herself) and what people will think of him (or her). Life can be challenging enough dealing with the devil, but the Bible says <u>God</u> resists the proud. That's not surprising when you consider that pride is of the devil, and we are held responsible for resisting the devil and his ways. If you don't resist the temptation to give in to pride, *God will resist you.* And if *God* is resisting you, whatever you are doing (including trying to receive the Holy Spirit) isn't going to produce results.

So if pride is a problem when it comes to receiving the Holy Spirit, repent right now of that pride. Humble yourself. Once you have begun to experience the baptism with the Holy Spirit, be willing to step out in faith boldly and speak in tongues audibly (loud enough to be heard). You don't have to yell, but speak at a normal sound volume, loud enough for you and a person standing next to you to hear. Don't worry about how you sound or what anyone else thinks. Just do it. You will see results.

5. You must be in fellowship with God. I mentioned earlier that salvation is basically the only requirement for being baptized with the Holy Spirit. One might argue that there are two requirements—being saved and being in fellowship with God. However, these two are so closely intertwined that rather than call these the No. 1 and No. 2

requirements, I'd rather call them Nos. 1 and 1A.

These two go hand in hand, because once a person is saved, he is in fellowship with God. That is, once a person receives the Lord Jesus as Saviour, at that point he is in fellowship with God. But though salvation and fellowship with God are related, they are not the exact same thing. It is possible for someone who has been saved to get *out* of fellowship with God. Sin takes you out of fellowship with God. Confessing your sin to God and turning away from that sin brings you back into fellowship with the Heavenly Father.

Fellowship is not the same thing as relationship. A son might get angry with his natural father and say, "I hate you. I'm not speaking to you." **At that point, fellowship is broken. But the relationship is still the same.** It is still a father-son relationship, even though the son is not on speaking terms with the Father. *Fellowship, in essence, means you and the Heavenly Father are on speaking terms.* You don't have to be perfect to stay in fellowship with the Father, but you do have to be quick to repent and ask forgiveness from the Father when you do sin. As long as you do that or are doing that, you remain eligible to be filled to overflowing with the Holy Spirit.

Some might argue that I'm trying to say that the Holy Spirit is not a free gift. That's not what I'm trying to say. The Holy Spirit is a free gift. But it's not a matter of earning a gift, but a matter of *staying in position to receive* the gift. Someone may want to give you a gift in Cleveland, but if you are in Tokyo, you are in no position to receive the gift. In order to be in position to receive the Holy Spirit, you must be in fellowship with God. You and the Heavenly Father must be on speaking terms. If unconfessed sin has broken that fellowship, repent right now. Confess your sin, turn from your sin, and turn to the Father. Get back in fellowship with your Heavenly Father.

6. There's nothing to be afraid of.

"If a son shall ask bread of any of you that is a father, will he give him a stone? Or if he ask a fish, will he for a fish give him a serpent?

"Or if he shall ask an egg, will he offer him a scorpion?

"If ye then, being evil (that is, natural beings capable of sin), know how to give good gifts to your children, *how much more* shall your Heavenly Father give **the Holy Spirit** to them that ask him." (Luke 11:11-13).

In short, this means if you ask the Father for the Holy Spirit, you have nothing to be afraid of. You will receive the Holy Spirit. God isn't going to give you anything else but the Holy Spirit. God isn't going to hurt you, or embarrass you, or give you a demonic spirit, or anything like that. You will receive the Holy Spirit, plain and simple.

When I first experienced the Holy Spirit baptism, fear gripped me. In my case, because I was being tormented by the devil, I was afraid not to receive. Others, often because they have been exposed to wrong teaching, are afraid to receive. Either way, fear is a serious hindrance.

Don't be afraid. The Holy Spirit won't hurt you. You won't be forced to speak in tongues every minute of every day for the rest of your life. You won't be forced to speak in tongues against your will. You have nothing to fear by receiving. And even if you have trouble receiving, don't give in to fear. Your eternal salvation doesn't hinge on the baptism with the Holy Spirit. But your overall spiritual well-being in this life is affected by it, so don't give up! Keep believing and acting on your faith until you get results! Which brings us to…

7. You must be in faith. You can't overlook this one.

"For without faith it is <u>impossible</u> to please him, for he that cometh to God must believe that He is, and that He is a <u>rewarder</u> of them that diligently seek Him" (Hebrews 11:6).

"Well, that rules me out," you may say. "I just don't have a lot of faith." I have good news for you. You don't *need* a lot of faith. You only need faith the size of a tiny grain of mustard seed to move any mountains in your life (Matthew 17:20). In other words, it's not as much a matter of how much faith you have, but whether you are using it or not. Do you believe God (regarding the Holy Spirit baptism and tongues) or not?

"Yes, I believe in the Holy Spirit baptism," you may say. "Yes, I believe in speaking in tongues." That's fine, but do you believe *you* can receive the Holy Spirit? Do you believe *you* can be filled? Do you believe *you* can speak in tongues? Be honest with yourself about these things.

If you have trouble believing that you can be filled with the Spirit, feed the faith you have by not only studying what the Word has to say about the Holy Spirit, faith, and tongues, but *meditating* on it (contemplating it out loud to yourself, chewing on it).

Joshua 1:8 instructs us to meditate on the Word of God. If you believe the Bible, then the more you meditate on what the Bible says about the Holy Spirit, faith, and tongues, the easier it will be for you to believe that you can (and will) be filled with the Holy Spirit, with the Bible evidence of speaking with other tongues. Remember that God is no respecter of persons (Acts 10:34), meaning that he doesn't arbitrarily play favorites. If anyone else has ever been filled with the Holy Spirit, that is proof positive that you too can be filled!

Having said that, now is your time.

Turn to the next chapter for further instructions, and prepare to be set free!

CHAPTER 12

It's Your Time!

You know you are saved. You know you are in fellowship with God. You know you believe the Bible. You realize that being filled with the Spirit is not the same thing as speaking in tongues. You realize that you are the one who will do the speaking, not the Holy Spirit (the supernatural part is *what is being said,* not who is saying it). You have humbled yourself. You are hungry for more of God. And you know there is nothing to be afraid of.

Assuming that all of these things are true, you are ready. It's your time.

If you have another Spirit-filled believer with you, it is certainly OK and scriptural for him or her to lay hands on you to receive the Holy Ghost. If no other Spirit-filled believer is present, it is still possible to be filled with the Spirit. But keep this in mind: Satan will most certainly challenge you in this area. No matter what happens, he will lie to you and say it wasn't real, or that you didn't receive, etc. So it is better to have another Spirit-filled believer present to encourage you, to read these instructions to you, and to confirm the legitimacy of your experience.

Pray the following prayer, essentially the same one as in

Chapter 10.

Father, I thank you for saving me from hell. I thank you for your son, the Lord Jesus Christ. I thank you for the Spirit of Christ that now resides in my heart. And Father, I now realize that in addition to my salvation, it is your desire that I be filled to overflowing with divine power. Father, I want that divine power. I know that I cannot live the kind of life that you want me to live without the infilling of the Holy Spirit. And so right now I purpose in my heart to receive the Holy Spirit; to be filled to overflowing with the Holy Ghost. Holy Spirit, come into my spirit right now, and fill me to overflowing with your presence. I thank you in advance. *I am receiving the Holy Spirit right now by faith.* In Jesus name I pray. Amen!

By this time the Holy Spirit is all over you! (Don't worry about whether you feel Him all over you or not. Just believe it, because it's true!) Now relax, open your mouth wide (as an act of faith), breathe in, and receive. Drink of the Spirit. Make sure that your mouth is prepared to speak (in other words, don't have your lips glued together so that only a crowbar could separate them). By this time, the Holy Spirit is forming supernatural words on the inside of you. You may even be able to hear those words forming inside your spirit being, as though they were just waiting to come up out of your belly. You may sense the Holy Spirit moving on those organs and muscles in and around your mouth (your jaw, your tongue, etc.). **All of this is normal, but unless you actually *speak*, in all likelihood nothing will happen.**

So, as those supernatural words begin to form, by faith draw them up out of your belly and out of your mouth, and speak those words. (Don't say anything in English, or in your native language.) It will seem like rivers of living water flowing out of you, and that's what it is! Let it flow! Don't stop it and start it; let it flow! You will hear supernatural words coming out of your mouth – words you never heard before in a fluent language which you have never spoken before.

Hallelujah! Glory to God! You are filled!

"But I don't understand what I'm saying!" you may say to yourself.

Your mind is not *supposed* to understand it. That is what makes it supernatural. It is the real you—your inner man, your spirit man (not your mind)—that is speaking supernaturally to God (I Corinthians 14:2). The important thing is that *God* understands it. And because you are speaking mysteries unto God, the devil *doesn't* understand it. Glory! Can you see how much more successful you can be in your prayer life by praying in the Holy Ghost? Praise God!

Now that you are filled, begin to live a Spirit-filled life. Continue to speak and pray in tongues on a regular (preferably daily) basis. I also encourage you to sing in tongues regularly; you will have some glorious times in the Spirit. Be willing to be used by God as a witness of Jesus Christ, and be ready to be used supernaturally in ways you never thought possible. Glory to God!

APPENDIX

Questions and Answers

While I am confident that many of you reading this have already been filled with the Spirit in the course of reading this book, I realize the possibility that some of you have not seen the manifestation of a fluent tongue yet. If that's the case, I encourage you to read this section, as well as the upcoming section entitled "A Final Word."

Question: *Are there any Biblical examples of a person who has been filled to overflowing with the Holy Spirit who didn't speak with tongues?*

Answer: Nope. In every instance in the Bible where someone has been *filled* with the Spirit (notice that I didn't say "has received" but *has been filled*), speaking in tongues is either mentioned (Acts 2:4; Acts 19:6) or implied (Acts 8:14-19). While speaking in tongues isn't always mentioned, you would have a hard time—in fact, an impossible time—trying to prove that there is even one Biblical instance of a person having been filled to overflowing with the Holy Spirit who did not speak with tongues. Keep in mind, though, that when I say this, I am speaking of human beings. Jesus Himself is a special case.

Question: *What about Jesus? Wasn't he filled with the Spirit? He didn't speak in tongues, did he?*

Answer: I don't see anywhere in the Bible where it says that Jesus didn't speak in tongues, but I would be inclined to agree with those who say he didn't. Even if that were the case, does that mean that we should not speak in tongues? Would that let us off the hook?

Not according to Jesus.

Jesus clearly said that believers would do the same works that he did, and *greater* works (John 14:12). No matter how you slice it, this indicates that Jesus is expecting us to do things that even *he* didn't do.

The late Kenneth E. Hagin, in his book *Tongues: Beyond the Upper Room*, noted that Jesus in his earthly ministry flowed in seven of the nine gifts of the Spirit mentioned in 1 Corinthians 12, but there is no clear evidence that he flowed in the other two—the gifts of "divers kinds of tongues" or "interpretation of tongues." Nor is there any evidence that those two gifts were in manifestation in the Old Testament. According to Hagin, the reason for this is because "these two gifts of the Spirit are distinctive of this Holy Spirit Dispensation, or age, which began with the outpouring of the Holy Ghost on the Day of Pentecost as recorded in Acts 2."

Those who are inclined to doubt what Hagin said regarding the "Holy Spirit Dispensation" would do well to pay attention to what the Bible says about the Holy Spirit, and in particular what Jesus himself said. Even if Jesus never spoke in tongues one day of his natural life, it is very clear to any honest person what his will is for the Christian:

"And these signs shall follow them that believe…they shall *speak with new tongues.*" – Mark 16:17, a direct quote from Jesus Christ himself.

"For John truly baptized with water, but ye shall be *baptized with the Holy Ghost* not many days hence." – Acts 1:4-5, another direct quote from Jesus.

"But ye shall receive power, after that the Holy Ghost is come upon you, and ye shall be witnesses. . ." – Acts 1:8, again a direct quote from Jesus.

And be not drunk with wine, wherein is excess, but *be filled with the Spirit.*" - Ephesians 5:18

"He that believeth on me. . .*out of his belly shall flow rivers of living water. . .*but this spake he of the <u>Spirit</u>, *which they which believe on him should receive*, for the Holy Spirit had not yet been given, because Jesus was not yet glorified." – John 7:38-39.

Anyone who has ever been filled with the Spirit with the Bible evidence of speaking in tongues knows that it is like "rivers of living water" coming up out of your belly. Jesus made it clear that anyone who believes on him should have rivers of living water flowing up out of his belly; in other words, they should be speaking in tongues. Hopefully by now that is obvious, but if you have any strong disagreements with that, you should take it up with Jesus, who said "them that believe. . .shall speak with new tongues. . ."

Question: *Didn't speaking in tongues go out with the early church? After all, 1 Corinthians 13 says tongues have ceased.*

Answer: No, it didn't go out with the early church; nor does the Bible say it ceased. The Bible doesn't say that believers will speak with new tongues for about 100 years, and then tongues will cease.

Some argue that tongues no longer exist based on a false interpretation of 1 Cor. 13:8-10. Let's take a look at this:

"Charity never faileth, but whether there be prophecies, they shall fail; <u>whether there be tongues, they shall cease;</u> whether there be knowledge, it shall vanish away. For we know in part, and we prophesy in part. But <u>when that which is perfect is come,</u> then that which is in part shall be done away."

"Well there you have it," some say. "That which is perfect (the Bible) has come. So that which is in part, including tongues, have ceased."

Give me a break.

The Bible is perfect, but that's not what's being discussed in 1 Cor. 13:8-10. It is Jesus, the Living Word of God, who is being discussed here. Jesus, the perfect, spotless Son, is coming back. *But He hasn't come back yet, so until He does, tongues are going to be here.* You might as well face it.

Sometimes the best way to prove that something is false is to assume that it is true. Let's assume that 1 Cor. 13:8-10 is trying to say that tongues have ceased. If that is true, we can also safely assume that knowledge has vanished away (1 Cor. 13:8). Has it? I think not. That pokes a big hole in the "tongues have ceased" theory.

Moreover, 1 Cor. 13:8-12 says, in effect, that now we know in part, but when that which is perfect has come, we will know "even as we are known"; in other words, since God knows everything about us, we will know everything about God and the things of God. If "that which is perfect" is the Bible, then that means we should know everything *now.*

I'm sorry, but speaking for myself, I don't know everything right now. And I don't know anyone who does. And just as partial knowledge hasn't vanished, neither have tongues ceased. You need to get that settled in your mind; otherwise you will never have the faith to ever speak in tongues, even though Jesus clearly indicated in Mark 16:17 that he is expecting you to do just that!

Question: *I noticed you never said anything about tarrying. Isn't it true that you have to tarry (or wait) to be filled with the Spirit?*

Answer: I never said anything about tarrying (or waiting) because it's not a requirement in order to be filled with the Spirit. And the Bible never says it is.

Now, I realize that some of you who grew up in certain denominational circles may take issue with that, but I ask you to hear me out, and also search the scriptures for yourself.

The Bible does say that Jesus asked his disciples, before ascending to the Father, to "tarry in the city of Jerusalem until (they be) endued with power from on high" (Luke 24:49). But after those same disciples were filled with the Spirit and spoke with tongues, it never says anything else about tarrying. According to Acts 10:44-48, Cornelius and the Gentiles were *immediately* filled, without waiting. According to Acts 19:1-6, the Ephesian disciples whom Paul ministered to were *immediately* filled, without waiting. Yet much of the church has built a doctrine around this "tarrying" concept, which shows the danger of basing an entire doctrine on only one scripture.

Let's face it—if there is even *one* person who has been filled with the Holy Spirit without "tarrying" or waiting, that proves that tarrying is not a requirement for receiving the Holy Spirit. If it were a requirement, everyone would have to do it.

If tarrying is so important, why stop at tarrying? Why not go the whole way with the scripture, and tarry in the city of Jerusalem? Before you start packing your bags for that long trip, I have good news for you. You don't need to go to Jerusalem. Nor do you need to tarry. You don't have to wait. You can believe and receive right now if you haven't done so already (see Chapters 8-12). If you haven't jumped on the bandwagon yet, now is a good time to do so. Go for it! Believe and receive!

Question: *According to 1 Cor. 12:10 and 1 Cor. 12:28-30, speaking in tongues is not for every Christian. You seem to be saying the opposite. What gives?*

Answer: I am saying the opposite. Not the opposite of the scriptures, but the opposite of the way the passages have been interpreted. The first passage (1 Cor. 12:10) doesn't say that speaking in tongues is only available to certain Christians. It does say that both the spiritual gift of "divers kinds of tongues" and the spiritual gift of "interpretation of tongues" are not available to every Christian. And that's true. But "divers kinds of tongues" is not the same as receiving the Holy Spirit with the Bible evidence of speaking with other tongues. "Divers kinds of tongues" and "interpretation of tongues" refer to the gift of tongues (as well as the gift of interpretation of tongues) as used in *public ministry*, while tongues in general are not for public ministry, they are for your *private* prayer life.

Before I comment on that further, let's take a closer look

at 1 Cor. 12:28-30.

"And God hath set some IN THE CHURCH, first apostles, secondarily prophets, thirdly teachers, after that miracles, then gifts of healings, helps, governments, <u>diversities of tongues</u>.

Are all apostles? Are all prophets? Are all teachers? Are all workers of miracles? Have all the gifts of healings? DO ALL SPEAK WITH TONGUES? DO ALL INTERPRET?

God has set some in the church. And 1 Cor. 12:28-30 begins with a list of who God has set in the church: first apostles, secondarily prophets, and so on. So the context clearly is *ministry*—specifically the *ministry gifts* that God has set in the church. In other words, anything in this passage has to be taken in the context of *ministry.*

"Are all apostles?" Not everyone is called to *minister* as an apostle. "Are all prophets?" Not everyone is called to *minister* as a prophet. "Are all workers of miracles?" Not everyone is called to *minister* the working of miracles. "Do all speak with tongues? Do all interpret?" Not everyone is called to operate in a *public ministry* that involves speaking in tongues and interpretation of tongues in the local *church.* That's what it is saying. It isn't even discussing the issue of speaking in tongues in your private prayer life, which is a separate issue.

For those of you who are still skeptical, you can debate this or argue about it all you want. But all you have to do is look at two passages in the Bible about tongues, and it is clear that two different things are being discussed. If you look at 1 Cor. 12:10, it says "to one is given this gift, to another that gift," and so on. If you look at Mark 16:17, it says "these signs shall follow THEM THAT BELIEVE...they SHALL SPEAK WITH NEW TONGUES," implying that speaking in tongues is a sign that should follow *everyone* that believes, not just one here, or another there.

You must keep in mind that 1 Cor 12:10 is referring to the gift of "different kinds of tongues" as they operate in public ministry. And 1 Cor. 12:28 is referring to a person who is used in the public ministry of "diversities of tongues." But Mark 16:17 is referring to speaking in tongues as your private prayer language, as the initial outward sign of being filled with the Spirit. And the infilling of the Holy Spirit is available to every believer, praise God!

Question: *Someone told me that if you haven't been filled with the Spirit, you're not saved. Is that true?*

Answer: No, it's not true. Some will argue that you need to speak in tongues in order to be saved based on Romans 8:9. This passage says, in essence, that if anyone doesn't have the Spirit of Christ, he is not saved. Well, that part is true. You must have the Spirit of Christ in you to be saved. *However, this verse is not referring to the baptism with the Holy Spirit.* It is referring to the baptism into the body of Christ, which is the new birth (See Chapter 2, The Doctrine of Baptisms). The Spirit of Christ is inside of every born-again believer, like an Alka-Seltzer tablet full of potential. That potential is activated to its fullest, however, when water is poured upon that Alka-Seltzer—in other words, when the believer experiences the baptism with the Holy Spirit, with the Bible evidence of speaking with other tongues.

Question: *I don't know about this "speaking in tongues" stuff. It seems like the people I know that speak in tongues commit sin just as much as other Christians, if not more. How can the baptism with the Holy Spirit be a legitimate experience when you have such poor examples of good Christian behavior?*

Answer: Believe me, regardless of how many Spirit-filled, tongue-talking Christians are living right or not living right, the baptism with the Holy Spirit is a legitimate experience.

You have to understand that once you are filled with the Spirit, that isn't the end. It is actually more of a *beginning*. You still have a free will. And you still have to deal with the devil. And you still need to know the Word of God and be able to apply the Word of God in order to live victoriously in this life.

Unfortunately, many who have been filled with the Spirit and speak in tongues do not attend churches that teach the full, uncompromising Word of God, so they are ignorant of their rights and privileges as a child of God. If they knew who they were in Christ, and knew the power of the Holy Spirit and the power of tongues, they could use that power to get sin out of their lives (see Chapter 7, Why Speak in Tongues). But because they don't know, they slip into a "just an old sinner saved by grace" mentality and live like sinners instead of like the righteous people that they really are.

Romans 5:17 says that those who receive the *free gift* of righteousness shall reign in life by Jesus Christ. If you are a Christian, a sinner is what you *were*. Righteous is what you *are*. You may be capable of sin, but because you are righteous, and because you have the power of the Holy Spirit at your disposal, you no longer are *bound* by sin.

Many, however, don't know this. So, tongues or no tongues, they are living sinful lives. It's sad. It doesn't mean that a person is not saved if they are bound by sin. But a Spirit-filled believer needs to live his life according to the Word of God if he wants to break that bondage. To continue in sin after receiving the Holy Spirit is a dangerous thing. Eternal rewards are being jeopardized. Even though speaking in tongues is a sign that provides added assurance of your own salvation, you don't want to live your life in such a way that causes you to doubt your own salvation, or even put that salvation in jeopardy. And living in sin takes you in that direction.

Even so, I believe that the Lord is raising up men and women who will be a testimony that they are not only filled with the Spirit, but that they are filled with the *Holy* Spirit (emphasis on the word "HOLY"). Hallelujah!

Question: *You mentioned earlier that there is a difference between receiving the Holy Spirit and being filled with the Holy Spirit (see Chapter 5). Is there also a difference between being filled with the Spirit and being baptized with the Spirit?*

Answer: I do not believe there is a significant difference between the two. Technically, it is possible for a glass in a bucket to receive water and be filled to overflowing with water, but not be fully immersed (or baptized) in water. However, if you take away the bucket that would hold the excess water, then it becomes evident that once the glass is filled to overflowing with water, the immersion of the glass in water has started, for all practical purposes. The overflowing water is beginning to immerse the glass in water. So these terms (fill and baptize), although slightly different, can be used interchangeably without much of a problem when referring to the Holy Spirit.

The terms "receive" and "fill" are also used interchangeably in the Bible, but I believe the difference between these two is somewhat more significant. The difference between a glass that is only one-third full or one-fourth full versus a glass that is filled to overflowing is a very noticeable difference. And a 12-ounce glass with only three ounces of water has indeed *received* water, even though it has not been filled to overflowing with water.

Question: *My Aunt Sally saw a beam of light right before she was filled with the Spirit. That never happened to me, so I must not be filled. Right?*

Answer: Wrong. Being filled with the Spirit has nothing to do with seeing a beam of light, or feeling a jolt go through the floor, or a lot of external signs. Aunt Sally may be telling the truth as far as what happened to her, but what happened to her has nothing to do with what has happened (or will happen) to you.

You have to understand that everyone's experience is different when it comes to the baptism with the Holy Spirit. Some people see things. Some don't. Some people feel things. Some don't. But regardless, we can't use someone else's experience as the basis for determining what our experience will be (or should be) like. Our only sure basis for determining what will happen with the Holy Spirit baptism is the Bible, which says in essence that the initial outward sign of being filled is speaking with other tongues as the Spirit gives the utterance (Acts 2:4).

Question: *Is it possible for someone to begin speaking in tongues before anyone ministers the baptism with the Holy Spirit to them?*

Answer: Yes. Absolutely. But keep in mind my answer to the last question: everyone's experience is different. Uncle Albert may have started speaking in tongues before anyone ever started praying for him. But there is no guarantee that your experience, or someone else's experience, will be the same as Uncle Albert's. The important thing to remember is this: *regardless of how it happens, every believer can be filled with the Spirit.*

Question: *Once you are filled and can speak in tongues, is it possible for you to ever lose that ability?*

Answer: If you are referring to a *fluent* tongue, I've never known it to happen. While it is possible (although it is extremely, extremely difficult) for a Christian to lose his salvation, I've never seen a Spirit-*filled* believer lose his ability to speak in tongues. The Bible says that the gifts and calling of God are without repentance (Romans 11:29), meaning that God doesn't take back the gifts that he gives. Jesus said "I will never leave you nor forsake you" (Hebrews 13:5). Even though we may be unfaithful, God never is (2 Timothy 2:13). *We may leave God, but God never leaves us.* Jesus said the Comforter (the Holy Spirit) would abide with us FOREVER (John 14:16). Forever is a very long time, praise God!

Now keep this in mind: if your tongue *isn't fluent to begin with*, and you don't spend time believing God to be filled to overflowing with the Holy Spirit, you may struggle for a while when it comes to speaking in tongues. But once that fluency comes, you will be able to speak in tongues from now until Jesus comes back, glory to God!

* * * * * * *

To summarize, we as Christians need the Holy Ghost, plain and simple. And we need the Holy Spirit in His fullness. Being filled with the Spirit, with the Bible evidence of speaking with other tongues, is a perfect example of "divine ability" being added to your natural ability. And that tandem, when combined with knowledge of the Word of God, will result in you gaining victory after victory in areas that you may have never thought possible.

So be filled! And if you have been filled, but your tank seems a little low, get filled again (you can get filled again, you know; it's like recharging a battery). Receive a fresh anointing of the Holy Spirit. Don't just be filled, but *stay* filled, praise God! Do that, and I can assure you that your life will never be the same.

A FINAL WORD. . .

Many of you who once had trouble receiving are now filled with the Spirit, with the Bible evidence of speaking in a fluent tongue.

But for those of you who are still having trouble, I want to reiterate that perseverance is the key. Don't quit. Don't give up. **If you apply the principles that you have read in this book, you can't help but to receive and to be filled with the Spirit.** You may have to reread the book three or four more times. You may have to reread Chapter 11 about seven times. But stick it out, because what you need is in this book you are reading right now.

If for some reason, you still are not confident that you are speaking in anything resembling a fluent tongue, it is important for you to persevere if you want to ultimately see the victory. In this case, that means you should thank God that you have indeed received the Holy Spirit in a measure, but declare to the Father that you desire to receive until you are *filled*. And receive some more. And speak some more. Remember, your faith is your inward evidence that you are filled with the Holy Spirit. *If you truly believe, then persevere until you see the outward evidence.*

Why do I say "receive some more"? Actually, if you are fully persuaded that you have received, and that is fully settled in your mind, then this step may not be necessary. I tell you to just keep speaking and trusting the Holy Spirit to give you the words to say, whenever you get the opportunity to spend time with God in prayer. It shouldn't take you very long at all to see the manifestation of tongues.

But if you are entertaining any doubts at all about whether you have received, then just "receive some more," remembering what I said about the glass that has received water but has yet to be filled with water. Receive some more (just like the glass) with the expectation that when you are filled to overflowing, you will speak in a fluent tongue. Do this without any reservations, and putting aside any doubts, and I guarantee you that your faith will be rewarded.

If you are fully grasping the principles that I'm sharing with you here, you'll be surprised at how quickly you see the manifestation of a fluent tongue.

But let's say you haven't fully grasped these principles. No worries. No need to panic. Even if you don't see that manifestation right away, and you go to bed that night not having experienced that manifestation, don't give up. Persevere. When you get up the next morning, set aside some time with God, and speak, trusting the Holy Spirit to give you the words to say. Continue to do this, like a glass that is being filled to overflowing with water, and do it with the expectation that the overflow (of supernatural utterance) will come out of your mouth. Speak in tongues by faith, expecting that overflow to come out of your mouth. And it will. Be assured that it will. Hallelujah!

Persevere. I can't emphasize that enough. Many Christians seem to lack perseverance when the things that they are believing for do not manifest right away. Stick it out, like it is a matter of life or death. (It isn't *literally* a matter of life and death, but treat it as though it is, because it is very important, spiritually speaking.) If you combine your faith with this type of perseverance, you simply will not be denied. Remember, if you have received the Holy Spirit, you have every reason to expect to speak in tongues, based on what the Bible says. Don't quit just because you don't notice it happening in the first couple of seconds, or minutes. Stick it out. You'll be glad you did, praise God!

Stay in faith, and when you see the victory in this area, be sure to praise the name of Jesus and be willing to share your testimony so that others may be set free as well.

Thank God for the Holy Ghost!

www.ingramcontent.com/pod-product-compliance
Lightning Source LLC
Chambersburg PA
CBHW061543050726
47593CB00002B/885